Plain Language Wizardry™

PLAIN LANGUAGE
LEGAL WRITING

Cheryl Stephens

Plain Language Legal Writing
ISBN 978-0-557-01450-7

© 2008 Cheryl Stephens
All Rights Reserved

Plain Language Wizardry Books
Vancouver, BC
PlainLanguage.com

Contents

Introduction: What is Plain Language?

Plain language is language that is clear and understandable — and as simple as the situation allows. Legal language that is plain poses special challenges, but is not impossible. Clearer, simpler writing — stripped of unnecessary complexity but not of style — will also help to improve your client relations.

What Is Plain Legal Language?

Plain legal language is language that is effective for its purpose and clear to the intended reader.

As a writer of plain legal language, your aim is always to be understood. Sometimes, you will aim to be understood by the ordinary reader, but not always. At times, you know you need only reach those who are familiar with the context and understand the terminology.

The Benefits of Plain Language

Confidence

Plain language inspires confidence in both the reader and the writer.

Clear writing is evidence of clear thinking; garbled thinking produces garbled language. If your thinking is clear, you can be confident that your written product will be of better quality than the average law office precedent.

Clients like to know what the documents you ask them to sign actually say:

- They can understand and act upon their rights and obligations when they receive advice and documents in plain language.
- They can make informed decisions and avoid legal complications. This inspires confidence in themselves and confidence in you.

The more experience a person has with lawyers and legal documents, the more likely it is that the person feels frustrated and angered by them. Why?

The more often a person deals with a lawyer or reads legal documents, the higher that person's expectation will be that they will acquire the skill to decipher legalese. Unfortunately, legalese is nothing more than incomprehensible legal language; that skill never comes.

So the client loses confidence in the whole process, in the lawyer, and in his or her own ability to function effectively in legal situations. By using plain language, you reduce your client's frustration and increase his or her confidence and rapport with you. This is bound to enhance your own confidence.

Cost-Efficiency

Plain language has made business and government more cost-efficient, and it can do the same for your practice. These are a few of the ways you and your clients save:

- You save valuable time in teaching your associates or students, and in editing or revising their writing.
- You save valuable time training legal assistants and other support staff. They are better able to understand and process clearer legal documents whether they are proofreading or working through administrative steps on a file. This gives them more confidence in their work and in the law firm. Such confidence produces more stability and lower turnover.
- You can eliminate many variables in document packages. You can simplify a document assembly by simplifying the documents themselves. Computerized plain-language precedent systems provide greater uniformity of service, confidence in the product, and a greater sense of security in your office.

Advance planning

Preparing plain language documents is advance planning for new legal requirements such as statutes governing consumer finance documents. Having plain language writing practices in place can save you from a rush or panic later.

Using plain language is also beneficial for many reasons:

- raises the firm's profile in the marketplace and attracts blue-chip clients,
- gives the firm a feature that distinguishes it from its competitors and provides tangible benefits to its clients,
- attracts new clients to the firm,

- gives the firm a new cultural focus: meeting client need,
- increases the firm's profits.

What to Expect Here

This work was first published in 1991. Much has changed in the world and in law practice. For one thing, plain language has gained wider acceptance since then, and overcome its critics. For another, we have learned that the average reader has less patience and lower reading abilities than was thought before the instigation of comparative international literacy surveys.

This edition of Plain Language Legal Writing is more focused than earlier editions on the tasks of writing to your clients or your public. I have learned much about this through 18 years of consulting, editing, and writing practice.

Drafting dispositive documents and development of forms will be left for others to discuss. But for quick gloss on it after a deeper analysis from someone else, read my *Crash Course in Plain Language Drafting*, available online at
http://cherylstephens.com/articles/

Cheryl Stephens
Vancouver, 2008

Part 1
Writing as a
Communication Process

You never merely write. You write to someone.

Henry Weihofen, in Legal Writing Style

Communication is not a one-way activity. You write in order to convey information to others. If your readers do not receive the message you intended to transmit, you have failed to communicate. Learning a few techniques can improve your writing efforts.

In the practice of law, often the most concrete product you deliver is a set of written documents. Whether or not the client achieves victory, the legal writer will be judged by the written product delivered and the feeling of the client that communication has been successful.

Legalese and Gobbledygook

Maury Maverick invented the word gobbledygook in 1944 to describe inflated, bureaucratic, impersonal writing. Such jargon produces cognitive closure in the average reader. In 1961, Henry Weihofen described gobbledygook's main attributes:

1. *It uses roundabout rather than direct ways of expressing the thought.*

2. *It prefers pompous or pretentious to simple expressions.*

3. *It makes excessive use of nouns.*

4. *The nouns it uses tend to be abstract ones rather than concrete.*

5. *It has a penchant for compound prepositional phrases.*

6. *It makes much use of the passive instead of the active voice.*

Henry Weihofen, Legal Writing Style

Plain language legal writing refers to legal writing that is well thought out, well organized, and understandable to the client without interpretation: the language is clear, the legal concepts are explained and the technical terms are defined.

Plain language is the opposite of gobbledygook or legalese, and you know it when you see it. This book aims to show you how to create clear and effective legal prose: plain legal language.

Even though your clients are paying for your legal expertise, surveys have shown that clients do make their decisions about future retainers based on lawyers' communication and interpersonal skills. Good lawyers are a common phenomena; good lawyers who are also good communicators are not.

The Legal Writing Institute, an international association of legal writing teachers and other writing experts, adopted this statement of support for plain language legal writing:

> *The way lawyers write has been a source of complaint about lawyers for more than four centuries. The language used by lawyers should agree with common speech, unless there are reasons for a difference.*
>
> *Legalese is unnecessary and no more precise than plain language.*
>
> *Plain language is an important part of good legal writing. Plain language means language that is clear and readily understandable to the intended readers.*

The Writing Process

So using plain language is desirable, but how is it done? These seven steps are all you need to take to write effectively:

> *1. Think about your reader and your purpose in writing. This may require research but will lead you to audience awareness.*
>
> *2. Plan how best to convey your message. This is your organizational phase.*
>
> *3. Prepare your first draft. This is the creation.*
>
> *4. Review your draft for common communication roadblocks. This is a general edit or revision.*
>
> *5. Prepare your edited version with care for technical factors. This is the technical edit.*
>
> *6. Use readers or other resources to evaluate your draft. This is testing.*

7. Reconsider your purpose, and the input you've received from other people, and revise your product again.

Inevitably, reviews will lead to changes. You will find yourself back at an earlier stage, reformulating and reconsidering your writing product. The writing process is like a spiral: the stages repeat at new levels until the desired result is achieved (or until you run out of time or money). It is said to be recursive.

Revision and Reorganization

Organizing information is the single most important thing you can do to make your writing readable. When editing, always reconsider your original plan of organization.

Having a descriptive introduction is helpful to the reader. It puts the main ideas in context and provides an organizational map for the document. Research has shown that readers jump to conclusions based on previous knowledge and expectations, and then read to confirm their own opinions. An introduction dispels reader preconceptions and lets the writer's ideas come through clearly.

Writing or rewriting the introduction after you have finished the document will improve it. Ensure at this stage that it depicts the actual content of your document. It may be easier to write the introduction after you have completed the full text, including a summary conclusion.

Chapter One
Plan, Research, and Prepare

Thinking is the first step in communicating. Successful writers devote the major portion of their time to the thinking or incubation stage. It is in this stage that you discover what your real message is and how you want to communicate it.

In this pre-writing stage you work out a plan of action to get the information to the reader in a way that they can make sense of it. You also visualize the final product.

How much time you need to do this depends on how much experience you have had with the type of writing project at hand. But remember you will always need to reinvent the product for each client and legal situation since you cannot rely on boilerplate clauses and precedent, or standard, forms.

In a major communications project, you can use part of the planning stage to consult with the people who will eventually read and use the documents under preparation.

Ponder and Research

Planning includes analyzing. Ask yourself these questions:

Subject: *What am I trying to say? Am I clear on the concept I want to communicate?*

Purpose: *Why am I trying to communicate this information? What do I expect my readers to do with this information?*

Readers: *Who are my readers? What are their interests? What do they know about the subject? If there is more than one group of readers, which group is my primary audience?*

Setting: *How and when is the document to be used? Are there any limits on its size?*

Constraints: *Am I under time pressure? On a limited budget? Am I serving a committee of differing viewpoints? How can I meet these challenges?*

The classical approach to writing has three pre-writing aspects:

- considering who your readers will be,
- figuring out what your reason is for writing,
- refining your message to suit the needs or expectations of your readers.

Today, especially in law offices, writing is a more focused and business-oriented activity subject to many limitations—on time, resources, and conflicting interests, to name a few. The last step in analyzing the communication task today changes accordingly:

- determining your constraints.

Decisions about form and content can only be made through an analysis that includes assessing the needs and abilities of the readers of the document. The analysis will lead you to the point where you can start preparing your first draft. You might apply this analysis to a client newsletter or to client aids.

Prepare and Plan

Artful writing requires preparation and a plan. Think about these aspects of the project:

Concepts

Who? What? When? Where? Why? How?

Focus

A means for generating ideas and refining your thesis

Research

Obtaining knowledge of the facts and the law

Tasks (the work elements)

- *delegation of aspects of the project,*
- *anticipating developments in production*

Organization (structuring the task and producing the document)

- *writers, editors, production staff*
- *norms of form and content*

What is your purpose?

When planning a legal writing project, it is helpful to think first of your own purpose in writing. Ask yourself this: Is my purpose to persuade, document, inform, or get action?

You should also ask yourself what your reader's purpose is in making the effort to understand your document. What does the reader want to know or do? The answer will give you a clearer statement of purpose.

Determine the constraints

Your planning must take into account the constraints you are likely to face. It is wise to identify the problems and face up to them at the beginning; they will not go away.

Common constraints affect writers in law offices:

- limited resources,
- time limits,
- protocols of drafting,
- rules of interpretation,
- settled or prescribed forms,
- negotiations incomplete or underway,
- word processing precedent systems,
- lack of substantive knowledge of law or facts.

Many lawyers cling to the wording of statutes or contracts when writing informational materials or reporting to a client. The task for those writers is to advocate for plain language in formal legal drafting.

It is important to identify problems so that you have potential solutions ready beforehand. These are common constraints:

- insufficient time, approaching deadlines, false urgency;
- inadequate instructions often not thought through properly;
- frequent variations in instructions;
- insistence on unnecessary detail;

- additional material and complex modifications late in the process.

Get organized

Once you have figured out your topic, thesis, purpose, audience, and potential problems, you can begin to plan your document in terms of its structure, layout, design, format, sequence, rhetorical pattern, and more.

You may alter your plan of organization several times before your writing project is concluded. So why plan it? You need to impose order on your thoughts and your document now, not later. Proceeding without this first plan of the final product can take you off on time consuming and wasteful tangents.

Use a checklist

Develop your own specialized checklist for any writing task that you handle often.

The local regulator of law practice may produce checklists that cover writing for particular legal matters. You can adapt these to develop a model of your own. A checklist is important because it acts as a reminder of the best process to follow. It frees your mind up to focus on the issue at hand.

Use a checklist rather than a previous document. A precedent form can become a straitjacket that limits your efforts to develop a document that suits the needs of the current client and circumstances. However, a precedent can be useful later, as a reminder later to bring forward additional considerations that you may have missed.

Prepare a first draft

Thinking and conceptualizing is the most important stage in a legal writing project, but you are courting disaster if you prolong it too much.

When you first receive a major writing assignment, note down the deadline in your diary. Next list all the tasks and steps you need to finish. Divide the available time into two portions: three-fourths for the preliminary stages and one-fourth for the writing stage.

Note the date that the writing stage must start in your diary, and be ready with an outline so you can start your draft by that date.

Write your first draft quickly. Do not edit while writing—you are basically laying down the foundation of your document. So don't second-guess yourself, and don't go looking for all the facts and that extra research. Write notes to yourself where you feel something has to be confirmed or researched, or leave blanks to be filled in later.

Overcome writer's block

Often at this stage the infamous writer's block makes its appearance. You may be unable to figure out where or how to begin—maybe because you don't have a proper plan or you haven't finished thinking through the issue. But if your time for planning is up, you've got to move ahead anyway.

Start anywhere in the document—wherever it seems easiest. You can always write your introduction last. But you need to get your ideas or information down on paper.

If your plan is sound, your purpose clear, and you know your audience, you're just stuck for motivation or inspiration. There are techniques that will help suppress your internal critic and get your ideas flowing:

Clustering

This is free-association — using diagramming and free writing — of ideas that develop from your topic phrase.

Branching

Take the seed of your idea and diagram a tree from it. Each related idea becomes a branch. Draw this like a picture. When it is finished, number the branches in order of priority and use this as your outline.

Brainstorming

Express any idea that comes to mind about your topic. Write down your ideas on the topic; don't stop to reconsider or to edit; keep generating ideas until the well runs dry.

Free-writing

This is like brainstorming but done on paper. Start writing about your topic and don't even lift your pen until you run out of ideas.

These methods will help you generate ideas and focus your topic and thesis. They may also lead you to the appropriate method of organizing your argument or document.

Outlining

One useful organizing step is creating an outline. Outlines are especially useful when you feel overwhelmed by the extent of your research. Outlining the document before beginning to write up your research clarifies and focuses the writing task.

Outlining, as you learned it in school, doesn't work for everyone — especially not for those who are intimidated by it or who let the outline become a straitjacket for their thinking. An outline works only if it is treated as a working tool, one that can be altered throughout the writing process.

You may find it useful to make an outline after you have written the first draft. This late outline can help to focus or clarify the relationships between ideas and the logic of their thesis.

Some writers find the technique helpful when they are reviewing someone else's writing, and finding problems with it.

One way to outline is to number the paragraphs, write a succinct summary of each paragraph, then review the outline to see if the logic holds and the thinking flows. The numbered list can be used to reorganize the material.

A Writing Strategy for Tight Deadlines

You often have to write something in a hurry to meet a tight deadline. It is important in that situation that you should devote 50% of your time to formulating the thoughts you want to express and working out your plan or outline before actually starting to write.

Take these steps when you get a rush assignment:

1. *Clarify the task.*

2. *Try to delegate aspects of the task.*

3. *Brainstorm about it in writing.*

4. *Break it down into discrete time components.*

If you see blank when the words are supposed to flow, try writing down your thesis sentence:

- the sentence that states the point you want to make in the letter, or

- the question you need answered or that will lead to an answer.

This serves as a reminder of your purpose and keeps your thoughts focused.

Also, you can jot down significant words, facts, or ideas that come to mind about the subject. Use this as a reminder while you are dictating or drafting. It can serve as a free-form outline of what you need to write.

When you set about writing, start wherever your inclination sets you—in the middle or at the end. Later, as your final step, you should go back and write or reconsider your introduction and your closing.

If deadline writing always makes you anxious, take this advice:

- Clarify your goal.
- Don't start writing until you have your orientation sorted out.
- Concentrate on your target and not on form and detail.
- Check form and detail at the end and try to involve another person in the final review.

Chapter Two
Tailor the Writing
to the Reader

Identify the Audiences

It is important to identify readers and be aware of their characteristics, needs, and expectations. But audience awareness becomes complicated when you are writing for more than one group.

In the law firm, you write to other lawyers, other professionals, government agencies, individual clients, business clients, and lay people who are not your clients at all. You write letters that may be read only by one person at one time. You may also write business documents or informational materials that will be used over and over by many different people.

Take the legal opinion letter for an example. It is written, first and foremost, for your client. But when writing it, you probably keep other lawyers in mind. And your client may circulate it to his or her own customers.

In commercial law practice, you deal with experienced professionals, small proprietors, and novices. In a government office, you may write to experienced lobbyists or to people who feel they are at the mercy of government. Each requires a different approach. You may not be able to meet the information needs of everyone in the same document.

Good lawyers learn to assess their clients' needs, abilities, comprehension levels, and psychology. Plain language writing requires you to apply such skills of assessment to determine what approach would work best for each communication project, and what types of documents are required to service readers.

You might be surprised to know how many different audiences read legal documents. Go beyond the primary audiences and you might discover a range of secondary audiences.

To find the secondary audience, you must research how documents are handled and processed by the organizations that use them. Still, your client is your primary audience or can identify the primary audience for you.

Select the most significant readers

Who will be the significant readers of these documents? Which readers should you have in mind when making decisions about what to say and how to say it?

The significant reader may be the reader who is least likely to understand your document. Write and design your document for this reader, if doing so will not alienate other audiences. If it might, then consider whether you actually need different documents for different groups of readers.

Can you use one document if you include a glossary of terms and concepts? Can you divide one document into sections addressed to different users?

If you must use one document, then you must decide which audience is the most important for the document, so you can plan accordingly.

Get to know your readers

Analyzing reader characteristics is not much different from evaluating people, and evaluating people is part of the lawyer's job.

Litigators evaluate how a person will perform as a witness: how well the witness communicates, and how he or she will be perceived. Litigators analyze judges, juries, and opposing counsel. They speak to juries differently than they do to judges. They change their tone and style from direct examination to cross-examination.

Lawyers analyze their clients in interviews:

- What does this testator really want?
- What is really important to this businessperson in this transaction?
- What is not being expressed here and why?

You have already learned how to tailor your message to your audience when talking face-to-face. You need to apply this type of analysis and responsive style of delivery when you are writing.

To get to know your reader, you may have to do some research; if your document is meant for a specific client, your research will focus on the client's needs. Some basic characteristics will be shared by all clients, and then there are the special characteristics of special readers.

While most people do not fit the old definition of illiteracy, many people are challenged by the task of reading. And they are unnecessarily challenged by legalese.

It is good practice to write as simply and clearly as possible. And design your page and organize your document well, to make reading it as easy as possible. This will help you communicate effectively with your readers.

Audience characteristics

You need to know the characteristics of the significant audience for your document. Gather information about your readers:

- age range
- gender identification
- marital status
- first language
- professional interest
- familiarity with law
- sensitivities
- familiarity with subject matter
- desire to participate
- attitude in the circumstances
- education and reading levels
- physical, mental or emotional problems
- profession or occupation

Legal Writing and Client Literacy

You have a business client. This client trusts others to handle all her legal documents and accounting. She expresses frustration over the paperwork. She asks to take an annual report home to study before she can sign it. Another client is at risk of losing his income because he is refusing job training, a promotion, or reassignment.

Such behavior may indicate a literacy problem.

If you give your client a legal document to read, does she read slowly and laboriously? Can she summarize what the document says? Has she filled in a form with the wrong information, or made mistakes in spelling or grammar? The problem may be that the client can't read well enough to understand the questions, or can't write well enough to answer.

One in five adults cannot read English. One in four can, but only simple material that is well laid-out. And one in three, though they have adequate reading skills for most tasks in day-to-day life, cannot cope with unfamiliar or complex information.

Law is a technical field. This means that many of your clients find legal writing difficult and, because it is important to them, frustrating. Only one in four adults can deal with your complex opinion letters or legal documents, and even they need the legalese explained.

Literacy is a law practice issue.

You can prepare for these situations by:

- identifying clients who may have trouble reading,
- adopting techniques that help these clients.

Some of your clients who usually perform at a higher literacy level will demonstrate *situational limited literacy*. Many factors can temporarily affect literacy:

- stress or psychology
- stage in life
- lack of practice or neglect

These added factors will affect client literacy in legal situations:

- pressure or stress over a legal matter
- intimidation by a situation
- legalese

Literacy is relative

To help clients who have reading difficulties, you need to be observant and aware. And cautious: adults with literacy problems can be embarrassed by people who make a big deal of their problem, or who talk about it in front of other people. It is likely that such clients didn't receive much support in the past when they revealed their low literacy skills.

They may have hidden this inability to read and write well because of the stigma attached to illiteracy—shielding their embarrassment behind anger or defensiveness.

Most lawyers wouldn't want to ask a client point-blank: "Can you read?" But there are clues that you can pick up when you suspect that a client is not able to read the legal documents you want read and understood.

Low literacy can be invisible. Low literacy is a problem that knows no age, education, economic boundaries or national origins.

How to help with the legal literacy problem

When you talk about the legal problem, repeat yourself. People who can't read pick up compensatory skills. They have well-developed memories and may use mnemonics—memory aids. They may ask you to repeat something so they can memorize it.

You can also help by finding new ways to convey information. Use plain language. People with lower literacy skills can only cope with written information that is simple and clearly laid-out, in language that is familiar and well organized.

Review your communication practices.

Chapter Three
Organize Both Content and Structure

Document Logic

You must be clear about how and why you have organized the document as you have, before you can make the logic behind the organization clear to your reader. Consider your organizing scheme for the document as a whole, for the separate parts of the document, and for the paragraphs in each part.

Here is a useful plan for organizing information:

1. *Create logical categories.*

2. *Divide the information among the categories.*

3. *Sequence or order those categories.*

4. *Divide and order information within the categories.*

When creating categories, the main principle is utility: What arrangement presents the information in the best light to suit your purpose (or your client's advantage)?

Four elements should be considered when making categories:

- nature of the subject matter,
- client's objectives and needs,
- purpose for organizing the information,
- strategy chosen in the legal matter.

Legal writing expert Reed Dickerson identified the most common categories in legal drafting:

- kinds of person affected,
- administrative organizations involved,
- fields in which they operate.

Dickerson suggested that systems like chronology be used for secondary divisions within categories rather than as primary categories.

Document logic determines document structure. Both logic and structure develop from your purpose and the legal strategy that serves your purpose.

The structure of your document should correspond with the problems it is intended to solve for the reader—and it should start from the vantage point of the reader.

The real world being what it is, there are some indivisible subjects which will not fall clearly into one category or another, or seem to be pulled in two directions. This calls for an almost arbitrary decision on which category is more suitable for your subject but the decision should favor the reader's sense of logical relationships.

Legal writers may have many purposes to cover. But the foremost or overall purpose of a legal document is usually to explain, persuade, respond, narrate, or prove something.

These are strategies writers can use to accomplish their purpose:

- define
- classify
- compare
- evaluate
- contrast
- show cause and effect

Perspective

In choosing categories, also consider the different levels or perspectives from which you can address the topics.

This is like choosing between first-person, second person or third-person perspective when you construct a sentence, only here you must do so for the whole document and its parts. Disorganized writing often flows from a constantly changing perspective within topics and even within paragraphs.

Consider organizing and dealing with your information from one of the following perspectives:

client – *your client or the other lawyer's client, someone who does something or has it done to them*

object – *that thing or idea which is the basis of the matter or concept*

principle – *the law and moral or ethical issues*

lawyer – *you as writer, your firm, your role in the progress of the matter*

reader – *the "you" who will read the document, whether your client or the other lawyer or the judge*

Different levels or perspectives have some uses: they can serve as the basis of your secondary division within categories. It is important for you to recognize the different levels and use them consistently from one category to the next.

Outlining as an Organizer

You might find it helpful to have an informal, working outline at this point in the writing project. The outline may change in the course of working out the full logic and exploring the ideas, but it will provide a roadmap for your thinking and writing.

Once you have the document logic worked out, use it to prepare your table of contents and to work out your topic headings in an outline. Remember that the outline headings may not be suitable headings in the end, but if you set them up in the draft, they can be revised later.

Logical Sequence

Systems of division and sequencing

Once the information is divided into categories, the categories must be ordered in some way. The following systems are sometimes appropriate for sequencing information:

> most important to least important—*This is the most common system and is particularly helpful if you are dealing with a long and complex document.*

> general to specific—*This is useful where you are presenting exceptions to the rule. State the rule or principle first and then give exceptions or explanations of how the general rule is applied in a specific context.*

> chronological—*This is useful to develop or present a story or history of events.*

alphabetical—*This is useful with a lot of diverse information, as secondary divisions under primary categories.*

substantive to procedural—*This is traditional in legislation and contracts.*

Consider alternate patterns

Use a sequence logical to your audience or material.

Lawyers often think there is only one logical way to organize information. For example, many lawyers believe that the traditional organization of statutes is the only logical organization. Beware of such legal-blinders when organizing material.

What organization works best for readers? What questions are on the mind of the reader?

Secondary level

Organize the document by sequencing the paragraphs. Put the most important things first. There will be a higher rate of recall, and it is a means to prioritize their value.

Another way is to describe the rule or main principle first, then follow with the qualifiers and exceptions.

Conscious Structure

Begin with an overview

Use the first paragraph to explain what and why you are writing. Use the next paragraph to summarize your conclusions or outline the topics you will discuss.

Long, windy introductions are not good, but some lead-in is necessary to focus the reader's attention. An introduction should help readers to put the main ideas in context.

A typical newspaper lead sentence introduces the who, what, when, where and why of the story. Your lead should explain what kind of document this is and why you are writing it, and give the basic facts that the readers need to have before they proceed.

The reader should not have to go looking for another document to get the facts needed to read and understand your document.

The lead-in to your document can also serve as a transition from the reader's perspective and preconceptions to your conception of the issues. It thus allows you to steer the reader from erroneous assumptions. The lead-in should include a clear summation of your position or conclusions, and dispel any preconceptions. This will enable your own ideas to come through clearly.

Prose outlines

If the document surveys several topics or it doesn't end with a conclusion, the second paragraph should serve as a prose outline or table of contents for the remainder of the material. This may be no more than a list of your major headings.

Example

On the basis of these facts, this memo will cover the following topics, which fall within the ambit of my instructions in this research:

1. When is there is a conflict of names between two companies?

2. Who determines if the conflict is actionable?

3. What is the procedure to seek an order for a change of name?

4. What is the mechanism for appeal?

Use signposts to show the structure

It is common to use these titles when organizing a legal document:

Introduction

Part 1

Part 2

Part 3

Conclusion

However these titles give no hint about the nature of the parts or the content of the document. Giving non-descriptive titles to the parts—even titles such as *Facts, Law, Conclusions*—is a waste of time. These are useless as headings and in outlines. The best choice for a heading is a word or phrase that describes the information in the text to which it belongs.

Use descriptive headings

Use headings that are meaningful, that describe the content of the material that follows or that ask the questions that the material answers. The appearance of the heading should signal the importance of the divisions in the overall document.

This subject is discussed in the chapter on design and layout.

The most important heading is the title of the document. It should be an accurate characterization of the document and should use the normal meaning of a word—don't call a document a mortgage if it is a guarantee.

Use headings to show document logic

Think of headings as a flow chart. Headings lead the reader from main points to subordinate points and mark new topics. They can work like a skeleton to hold the body of your work together.

Headings can serve several purposes:

- lead the reader to another topic,
- be descriptive and predictive,
- show readers where a pause is suitable,
- break up the document into manageable pieces for serial reading, and
- act as an internal index helping readers to find important information within the document.

Chapter Four
Edit, Peer-edit, and Test

In the law office, preparation of legal documents is often accomplished through teamwork. A team consists of senior counsel, associates, students, and paralegals, along with the senior counsel who is expected to do major editing. When you have the chance, it is better to allow your peers or supervisors to edit your writing; you can do the same for others—and present the senior counsel with more impressive drafts.

The law firm benefits from having someone other than the author review a draft for continuity and uniformity, as well as to tighten and streamline. A colleague's review will improve legal accuracy as well.

Editing Other Writers

Criteria for changes

When reviewing someone else's writing, consider any objective criteria that have been established: a firm style guide, a drafting checklist, and a binding authority. These resources not only provide you with a guide for editing, they serve as independent, neutral authorities. Your editorial suggestions will not appear to be arbitrary preferences.

Reader sensibilities or comprehension should be the next motivation for changes in the document. If the intended reader won't understand it or see the logical connections, change is necessary, but be sensitive to the writer's sense of identification with the written material. Don't let your editorial comments become insulting.

Be sensitive to writer's ownership

If time constraints do not permit discussing the changes with the writer immediately, sit with the writer later and discuss the necessary changes in the document.

Try to find something positive to say before launching into your constructive criticism. If you particularly liked some aspect, say so, but remember that praise should be sincere or it will sound hollow.

Edit the work of others with a pencil. You can then erase and rewrite freely and not have to worry about the writer's sensitivity to having a work marked with a lot of red ink. Mark your changes neatly, so they are easily read.

Use a system

Most inadequacies in writing fall into one of two categories: overall organization or prose style. Tackle the general considerations first: content, organization, tone. Comment on technical writing matters last.

Effective editors have their own system—any system that works for you is better than no system at all.

One system for checking organization involves making an outline of the document after-the-fact. An outline can help you check for logical development, parallel treatments, missing sections, and proper transitions. The outline can be produced from the headings and subheadings in the document.

If the organization remains a mystery even after this exercise, write a one-sentence précis of each section, review the topic development, and put these in proper order.

If these methods don't help make clear the organization of the issues or logical development of an argument, suggest that the writer make an outline of what he or she has written. The two of you can then work with the writer's outline to put things in a more understandable order. You can use the writer's outline as a roadmap when you are revising the document.

Once you have made the needed changes in organization and logic, then consider the grammar, sentence construction and vocabulary. At this point, you may find an editing checklist helpful. A checklist, like a system, reminds you to follow a minimum procedure.

Examples of editing checklists can be found on the Internet:

http://www.illinoistrialpractice.com/2008/03/self-editing-ti.html

http://www.gmu.edu/departments/writingcenter/handouts/check.html

http://search.ssrn.com/sol3/papers.cfm?abstract_id=1130308

Get Help From the Writer

If a sentence is too complicated to unravel, ask the writer to try to explain it to you. The writer should then rewrite the material just as it was explained. Another technique is to read the document aloud to listen for things that don't sound right.

If the content itself seems unfocused, discuss the following questions with the writer to clarify and focus the content:

Who are your readers?

What are you trying to say to them?

Why are you trying to communicate this information?

The Last Check

Software can eliminate some embarrassing errors made by writers and overlooked by editors. Use your spell-checker—a mandatory step in the production process that is often forgotten. But the spell-checker is not sufficient, because it only checks spelling and cannot catch errors in choice of words. For example, a spell-checker will accept "not he" in place of "not the," and "their" in place of "there." Many writers also benefit from using grammar-checker programs as well, though only some of the program's suggestions will be useful.

Punctuation errors can be spotted during proofreading. Some word-processing programs can catch inappropriate use of some punctuation, such as dashes and colons. Reference guides are also useful when the writer and editor cannot agree on the correct punctuation.

Proofreading your final copy is also mandatory.

Changes can crop up where you least expect them in the course of minor revisions elsewhere in the document. In *Elements of Editing: A Modern Guide for Editors and Journalists*, Arthur Plotnick advocates having a document proofread four times. He claims that two times will uncover 99% of the errors, but total accuracy requires two more times.

An important document should be read aloud to the person checking the document as it is read.

The writer has read and rewritten the draft several times. The senior lawyer has read it once or twice in different editions. Both are familiar with the material or their intentions for it, and will read in things that are missing. It is worth your while having another person go through it with fresh eyes, to proofread for punctuation, spelling, capitalization and formatting, and to check figures, names, titles, citations and mathematical computations.

A Caution on Precedents

It is a mistake to use wording from a precedent if you do not understand the meaning and effect of the wording. You should never assume that a precedent is adequate for your needs, even if that precedent is commonly used in the legal community or in your office.

An effective way to edit a precedent written in out-dated legalese is to follow this two-step process:

> First, *rewrite the material in your own words to confirm that you understand its meaning and effect.*

> Second, *edit and revise your version for clarity and conformity with the firm's official style.*

In working with precedents, you will often find gaps, omissions, and ambiguities that have been overlooked in previous uses. By revising and updating the material, you are actually making it more accurate and effective.

When you are drafting fresh material, it helps to look at a precedent after your first draft—to check if you have missed any common components.

Often formbooks containing precedents and model agreements also have checklists for contents. Review and use these checklists when appropriate.

Test a Document on Your Client

Some types of documents are for distribution to people other than your client. Go over the document with your client. Not only will your client appreciate the collaborative effort, you can ensure that you have fulfilled the client's instructions.

If the client can't understand words or concepts in the document, these ought to be changed or defined. If you can't explain words or concepts satisfactorily, perhaps you will remember not to put anything in a document when you don't know what it means!

If your instructions were not clear, this is also an opportunity to clarify the client's intentions.

Materials that will be reproduced by the client for use by customers or staff should be tried out on that audience to determine if they will understand. A document meant for distribution to the public should be tested on members of the public before the final version is printed.

Testing the document will disclose whether it is:

- comprehensible to the intended readers,
- user-friendly for the person who will fill it out or sign it,

- user-friendly for the people who will process it,
- legible, efficiently laid-out,
- complete for its purposes,
- simple to read,
- attractive to potential users, and
- capable of achieving the desired effect.

Part 2
Writing to Be Understood

The actual writing phase began when you prepared a first draft. But at that point you were merely trying to record your ideas.

Always reshape your draft to match the needs and abilities of your target audience; a competent writer is one who can do this quickly and efficiently. With experience, you can anticipate the reader's concerns, and address them early in the process.

The goal is to express simple ideas clearly, and complex ideas as precisely and simply as possible. Writing expert Joseph Williams describes the problem you face in trying to improve your mode of expression:

> *Whether we are readers or writers, teachers or editors, all of us in professional communities must understand three things about complex writing:*
> - *it may precisely reflect complex ideas,*
> - *it may gratuitously complicate complex ideas,*
> - *it may gratuitously complicate simple ideas.*
>
> *Joseph Williams, Style: Toward Clarity and Grace*

The chapters that follow show how to simplify language and expression. The clarifying effect on your writing will be cumulative.

The rules set out here should not become clichés of style, but guidelines for improvement. The essential ingredient is thoughtful consideration of your reader.

Chapter Five
Choose Your Words Wisely

Which Words Speak Directly to Your Readers?

> *Don't be afraid to sound like a lawyer, but try not to sound like the popular stereotype of a lawyer.*

Henry Weihofen, Legal Writing Style

In a study for the Law Society of British Columbia, the Continuing Legal Education Society asked clients about the readability of lawyers' retainer letters. The following commonly used words were problematic for clients:

paralegal

legal fees

deliveries

registry searches

out-of-pocket

enforcing

contingent fee

conduct of a lawsuit

litigation

parties

order

damages

settlement

appeal

conflict of interest

diverge

interim application

examination for discovery

Readers prefer familiar and concrete words. They prefer simplicity and consistency. They prefer genuineness to pretension, modern expressions to archaic words.

> *Style must be clear, as is proved by the fact that speech which fails to convey a plain meaning will fail to do just what speech has to do. Clearness is secured by using the words... that are current and ordinary.*
>
> *Aristotle, Rhetoric, The Words of Aristotle, W. Ross, ed. 1946*

While you struggle to clarify your meaning, keep in mind the level of simplicity and formality that is appropriate to the particular document and for the particular reader.

The last refuge of a sloppy writer is the excuse, "But my clients prefer formality" by which is meant pompous, inflated language:

> *Terminate* instead of *end, stop, finish, or close*
>
> *accede to* instead of *agree, give in, or comply with*

Use word pictures

Scenarios, analogies, metaphors, and similes paint a better picture in fewer words—a picture with vitality and color. They can make abstractions easier to understand. Just be sure you compare like things, you avoid clichés and platitudes, and you choose words that clarify meaning for your reader.

Readers whose first language is not English and those from other English-speaking countries may not be familiar with the reference. It is surprising how often we use metaphors (and mix our metaphors) without realizing it:

> *The **bears** would have us believe the sub-prime credit **virus** heralds the **end of the world**. They are wrong. The stock market—which I still believe is the best **barometer** of the **health** of business and the economic future—has behaved surprisingly well during this difficult stretch of **turbulence**. Yes, profits are getting **sloppy**. And yes, there are some credit **shocks out there** yet to be **revealed**. The **animal spirits** may have had their **wings clipped** a bit by the credit **crunch**, but there is still plenty of **sizzle** and **juice** in that story. It's very easy to be totally pessimistic and **bearish** right now. That is precisely why I will avoid **falling into that trap.***
>
> *Larry Kudlow,* National Review Online, *Sept. 14, 2007*

Avoid unnecessary repetition

Legalese, that special dialect of legal language, has a preference for using more than one word where one will do. This results from tradition or laziness.

Using phrases like these, you repeat yourself:

act and deed

goods and chattels

fit and proper

contract or agreement

null and void

fair and equitable

Such combinations are usually tautologies: needless repetition of the same idea.

Tautologies should be eliminated because they make your writing wordy and tiresome:

represents, warrants and covenants

representations, understandings and agreements

right, title and interest

in truth and in fact

referred to as and called

without let and hindrance

Latin was the language of law before the Norman Conquest of England in 1066. Afterwards, French became the dominant language of education, culture, and law. English survived amongst the population and later prevailed.

In 1362, the Crown decreed that oral pleadings in court should be in English. Later English was required in statutes: in 1731 in written pleadings. This is how the combinations of Latin, French and English words came to be used to express meaning with greater certainty—a habit that is clearly out-of-date.

Don't Use Problematic Vocabulary

Linguists consider legalese a separate dialect or class of language. Indeed, legalese is a kind of group slang, easily replaced with more modern vocabulary and form. Law does not need a separate language or a different dialect.

The first rule of legal interpretation is to look for the plain meaning of the words—that means looking first in a conventional dictionary, not a legal dictionary, nor a compendium of words and phrases that have been judicially considered. And if the dictionary provides a definition that is sufficient to answer the legal questions, that does it.

Some writers are using the following disclaimer to ensure that the plain meaning of the words is binding, although it should not really be necessary:

> This [document] is written in plain English, in an effort to make it understandable to persons who are not lawyers. Legal terms of art are used where necessary, but unnecessary legal jargon is omitted. This is an attempt to make the [document] clearer, not to change its effect.

Unnecessary jargon

This dictionary definition of jargon applies to legalese:

> The specialized or technical language of a trade, profession, or similar group. See synonyms at dialect.

*Speech or writing having unusual or pretentious
vocabulary, convoluted phrasing, and vague meaning.*

> The American Heritage® Dictionary of the English
> Language: Fourth Edition. 2000

A simple test for distinguishing necessary technical language
from unnecessary jargon is to try to express the idea in language
you might use with an intelligent listener in polite company at
dinner. If you can say it in plain English during a conversation,
why not write the same way?

Why not revise like this:

Traditional language

*Mr. Dodd has not offered me any advice other than as to the
good standing of the company*

Plain language

*Mr. Dodd told me only that the company was up to date in
all its regulatory filings.*

Some specialized terms are used because they have always been
used, even though the necessity no longer exists.

Legal terms of art

Various legal terms that cause problems to the client may be
defended as terms of art when they are really legal jargon. The
challenge to you as a writer is to determine whether a particular
word is jargon or a legal term of art. Look at words like: fee
simple, tort, injunction, master and servant, and execution.

Is a particular word a legitimate term of art? Legal scholar
Robert W. Benson has a test:

*A genuine, technical term of art has an uncontroversial core
meaning that cannot be conveyed succinctly in any other way.*
> Robert W. Benson, "The End of Legalese: The Game is Over"

There are a few genuine terms of art among the trade jargon. Some words that Benson accepted as terms of art have since been replaced statutorily in many jurisdictions:

plaintiff = claimant, applicant

defendant = respondent

injunction = order of prohibition

Words and phrases are discussed in litigation, but few are litigated themselves. Case law shows that the meaning of the word always changes to reflect the particular circumstances of the case.

Foreign words, archaic words, and old formalisms

Don't use Latin and French words for which English equivalents are readily available. Falling back on archaic words and old formalisms shows laziness in writing style.

Traditional language

I hereby acknowledge receiving a copy of this retainer.

Plain language

I have received a copy of this retainer (or) I have a copy of this retainer.

Visual Aids

Sometimes visual aids, not words, are the best tools to convey information. Visual presentations can complement, even replace, textual descriptions.

Photographs, drawings, and illustrations can not only show what you mean to say, but shorten the number of words needed to say it. Tables and graphs are useful to present numerical relationships and statistical data. Formulas easily explain mathematical relations and processes.

Diagrams and maps can describe locations, routes and geographic regions better than words. Diagrams can also be used to convey concepts. A corporate lawyer might use a diagram of related companies to explore conflict issues.

Compound prepositions

Compound prepositions add extra words and make your writing overly formal. Use the simpler forms below:

Compound	*Simple*
as a means of	*to*
as prescribed by	*under*
for the reason that	*since, because, for*
in accordance with	*by, under*
in case of	*if*
in relation to	*about, concerning, towards*
in respect of	*for, about, of*
in the course of	*in, while, during*
in the event that	*if*
in the nature of	*like, about*
on behalf of	*for*
no later than	*by*
notwithstanding the fact that	*even if, despite*
pertaining to	*about, of, on*
prior to	*before*
provided that	*if*

Compound	Simple
pursuant to	*under, by, following*
relating to	*about, on*
subject to	*if, as long as*
subsequent to	*after*
until such time as	*until*
with reference to	*about, concerning*
with regard to	*about, for, on*

Chapter Six
Features of Poor Legal Style

There are many problems with legalese. This chapter looks at four particular problems:

- lack of clarity from ambiguity or wordiness,
- multiple negatives and overuse of qualifiers,
- nominalization and loss of agency,
- bias and stereotypes.

Lack of Clarity

Vague, ambiguous and abstract words

There is a difference. Learn to distinguish between ambiguity (semantic, syntactic or contextual), vagueness, generality and flexible words. Then eliminate ambiguity from your writing and use vagueness deliberately when it suits your purpose.

> **Abstract words** *express concepts that are not concrete, concepts like* equitable.

Vague words like nearby *and general words like* vehicle *are inexact. For example,* transportation *describes some means of conveyance, while a* motor vehicle *is an only slightly more specific term, to describe a conveyance that is motorized.*

A more precise word can be found to describe a motor vehicle: *car, motorcycle,* or *truck.*

Even the words *car, motorcycle,* and *truck* are generalizations. While they are more specific than motor vehicle, they are less descriptive than *station wagon, sports coupe, motorbike, Harley Davidson, pick-up truck, tractor-trailer.*

These are types of abstraction:

abstract concepts–cloud on title, floating charge

vague words–basis, situation, consideration, character, factor, degree, aspect, circumstances, facilities, variables

deliberately vague, flexible words–undue, adequate, incidental, relevant

Ambiguity

An ambiguous statement is one that can be understood in two or more possible senses. Ambiguity is to be avoided, but flexible words may be necessary.

Ambiguous words have more than one interpretation. If you know what the intent is, you sometimes read it into the ambiguous expression. But you cannot count on your readers making the same interpretation.

The first step in dealing with ambiguities is to identify them. If you have to assume the meaning, the statement is probably ambiguous. If you have to go back over a sentence and think about its meaning, it is definitely ambiguous.

When dealing with ambiguities, you must consider all the possible meanings. If you need to, consult someone who knows which is the intended meaning.

Semantic ambiguity

A semantic ambiguity exists where an expression acquires more than one meaning because the words can be interpreted in more than one way. If the meaning can be determined from the context, however, there is no semantic ambiguity.

For example, the word bear has several meanings, but the intended meaning can be easily gleaned from the context: to bear witness, to bear investigation, to bear close examination, to bear responsibility. Most ambiguous words are not so easily differentiated. In legal writing, why use words that require context for definition at all?

The phrase the "date of the demise" may have several meanings:

demise = death, lease, convey, conveyance, rent, transfer, grant, bequest, bequeath

If you deduce that the intended meaning was *lease*, you still have a problem:

to lease = *to give someone the use of property under a lease, or to obtain the use of property under a lease*

In the following example, both *extraordinary* and *necessary* cause problems for the reader because the intended meaning is not clear:

Employees shall be only reimbursed for extraordinary personal expenses such as necessary wearing apparel.

There are two ways to tackle semantic ambiguity:

Choose a different, more exact word.

Define how the word is being used for your (immediate) purposes.

Syntactic ambiguity

A syntactic ambiguity is caused by poor grammatical structure in a sentence.

Often adverbs and adjectives are not placed adjacent to the words they modify. If you do not place the words properly and effectively, confusion results. Put your adverbs and adjectives as close as possible to the words they modify. The same advice goes with adverbial and adjectival phrases.

These sentences suffer from syntactic ambiguity:

The Plaintiff struck her head against the windshield and cracked it.

The bondholders of companies in the state shall register their bonds.

John looked at the person eating the sundae with wide eyes.

The solution to a syntactic ambiguity is to restructure the sentence.

If you have trouble identifying the problem, read the sentence aloud. If you stumble over a word or phrase, you've probably found the problem. Recast your thought as though you were explaining the matter orally to someone you know.

Or you could update your grammar skills online.

Contextual Ambiguity

A contextual ambiguity arises when there are contradictions or inconsistencies within a document or between related documents; the ambiguity comes from the context.

Use a different word only when you mean something different. When you have provided a definition for a word, don't use the word for a meaning other than the one you have given it in the definition. Do not change words for the sake of elegant variation.

General wordiness

Using too many words to say something can be as confusing as using misleading or vague words. Wordy writing is tiresome for the reader and forces the reader to struggle to sort out its meaning. Remember, it is never a compliment to say that someone is verbose.

Introductory phrases and transitional phrases can give your sentences style and cohesiveness. But all too often, legal writing is full of stuffy phrases. An example of wordiness is the following discussion of reasonable notice in contract clauses:

> It may be supposed that some clauses are so unreasonable
> that no practical means exists of giving sufficient notice. It
> becomes clear at this stage that the courts are using the
> requirement of notice in effect to strike down unreasonable
> clauses. With the development of a doctrine of
> unconscionability it is to be hoped that this function might
> be performed more directly...

Providing clarity

Make abstractions concrete

The law is full of abstractions, so you must make an effort–for your clients and other readers–to express these ideas as concretely as possible. This may mean using definitions to explain concepts or figures of speech to draw a word picture. For example, after using "color of right" add "belief in or appearance of a claim to right"; after using "cloud on title" add "for example, a claim of aboriginal title hovering like a rain cloud over your clear title to the property."

Use more precise words

Depending on the circumstance, choose the most precise word available. Follow these guidelines to avoid ambiguity:

- Choose the word that accurately describes what you want to say.
- Define terms.
- Use words consistently.
- Repeat the right word (don't use different words).
- Use a thesaurus or dictionary when you write.

Use flexible or general words if needed

There is a difference between vagueness and generality.

Vagueness is appropriate only in circumstances where a flexible meaning is required. But a general word is applicable widely. It is not flexible, but wide in its effect.

If your reasons are sound and you are acting within the scope of your client's instructions, you can use words that are flexible. Here are some flexible words and phrases used deliberately in law:

substantial performance

satisfactory conclusion

fit for the purpose

reasonable doubt

reasonable limitation

abuse of discretion

adversely affected

clear and convincing

contemporary community standards

custom and usage

fair division

moral turpitude

willful misconduct

Purposeful ambiguity

Some lawyers argue that there is a need for creative vagueness that allows room to maneuver a client out of obligations. Deliberate vagueness can also be allowed when a letter is a step in negotiations if the clients can't agree on more specific or detailed terms at the time but are eager to do business.

Use vagueness where appropriate, but stay on the lookout for unintentional vagueness and ambiguity.

> *"If I take refuge in ambiguity," Kingman Brewster, former president of Yale University, is reported to have said, "I assure you that it is quite conscious."*

Negativism

Multiple negatives

Try to construct your sentences with positive words. To understand a sentence containing a negative, the reader has to form the positive idea first and then convert it to the negative.

In spite of grammar school warnings about using double negatives, lawyers continue to use them. This example may not be grammatically wrong but it takes too much effort to balance:

> *There must be sufficient proximity between the parties that it would not be unjust or unfair to impose a duty of care.*

A multiple negative arises when words like absent, deny, fails, or false are combined with a word with a negative affix, like unwilling or careless or a negative word like no, not, never. Multiple negatives require mental gymnastics, and are to be avoided at all cost.

Consider the loops needed to sort out this sentence:

> *The failure to disclose an absence of reasonable cause is fatal to a claim for malicious prosecution and negligent investigation.*

Negative words like the obvious *no, never,* and *not,* are not the only culprits. Some words have negative implications that complicate a sentence when they are layered one upon another. Such words are: *none, unless, until, fail, exempted, unlawful,* and *invalid.* Like multiple negatives, layered negatives are a *no-no.*

The words with negative nuances are italicized:

Negative

> *This policy shall not be valid unless countersigned by our authorized representative.*

Positive

This policy becomes valid when signed by our representative.

Some negative prefixes and words are:

dis-	ex-	il-	im-
ir-	inmis-	non-	un-
fail	none	less	unless
until	absent	invalid	avoid
contrary	fail	delinquent	deny
doubt	except	lack	forbid
null	limitation	exempted	remote
unlawful	minimum	prevent	sanction

no less than,   no more than,   no smaller than

Some legal concepts indirectly express a negative. Be careful not to layer more negatives over them:

testimonial privilege

legally blind

volenti non fit injuria

constructive (possession, notice, etc.)

In this example, the construction of the sentence slows down the reader's comprehension:

Traditional language

Where the statute required that the vote of each board member be recorded, the absence of any record of a dissenting vote indicated an affirmative vote.

Plain language

Where the statute required that each member's vote be recorded, an affirmative vote was presumed if a dissenting vote was not recorded.

Now consider the accumulation of negative effects in this:

The oft repeated stricture that delegated power may not be exercised in a discriminatory manner is common cant in public law pleadings. Indeed, the routine repetition of the bare principle, unaccompanied by more, has become almost ritualistic. Such retreat to mere incantation is not surprising, absent a coherent line of judicial authority necessary for the progressive evolution of a principle fully formed by the rigors of case analysis. Whatever the transgression embodied in the ground of discrimination, it has been obscured by conflicting and confusing characterizations of the nature of the impropriety, with the result that judicial applications of the discrimination ground to the varied acts of public authorities have yet to reveal the substance behind the form. Except in its popularly recognized manifestations (now the subject of human rights legislation and the constitution) discrimination as a common law challenge to the exercise of delegated power continues to elude definition.

In the paragraph above, you might find it useful to identify the words with negative connotations by underlining them.

Qualifiers and contingencies

Multiple qualifiers can produce a result similar to that produced by multiple negatives: Without a prominent, positive assertion, a list of qualifications creates a negative. Some legal sentences set out all the exceptions before mentioning the general rule or assertion. It can be difficult to discern a rule when it is buried.

A listing of contingencies can also undermine your assertion. To persuade or argue effectively, state your position then address limitations. Eliminate contingencies and qualifiers that are irrelevant or unlikely to strengthen your main point.

To assert something, state it positively. Don't use negative form to make an assertion, even when you are on the defensive. And don't try to negate an opponent's argument before it has even been raised, forgetting to make your own positive assertion first.

Nominalization and Loss of Agency

Write with action

Compose sentences that have people doing things.

Readers look for the verb to understand what is happening. Action turns abstract when a verb is turned into a noun (called nominalization). The replacement verb, which is still a necessary ingredient of the sentence, is often a passive one. This worsens the problem.

When you say "a decision was reached by the Court" instead of "the Court decided," you have nominalized the verb *decide*.

If you "state the facts" for your opponents, you are being a more active participant in events than if "a factual statement is provided them."

> ### Traditional language
> *Consideration was given to provision of authorization for the execution in advance of their discussions.*
>
> ### Plain language
> *They considered whether or not to authorize the signing before they talked.*

Traditional language

The government's investigation into the methodologies used by the evaluators in the program survey analysis was met by their refusal in regard to an examination of their documentation.

Plain language

The government investigated the methods the evaluators used when they analyzed the program survey, but the evaluators refused to let the government examine their documents.

Change nominalizations to verbs

Putting people in your sentences solves many stylistic problems.

Removing nominalizations will lead you to correct many other problems with sentences, like overuse of passive verbs and wordiness. You can practice finding nominalizations by looking for words ending in *-ion*, *-ment*, and *-ence*.

Here are some commonly used noun forms of verbs:

Noun form:	Verb:
action	act
administration	administer
application	apply
cessation	cease
determination	determine
institution	institute
justification	justify
notification	notify
provision	provide

recommendation	*recommend*
requirement	*require*
utilization	*use*

Use active instead of passive voice

Verbs with active voice express action. Active voice is easier to read, uses fewer words than passive voice, and makes your writing stronger, clearer and briefer. Active voice moves the action toward the object of the sentence.

A passive verb directs the action back from the object to the subject. If the subject is performing the action in the verb, you are using active voice.

Active voice

Provincial court judges decide the traffic cases.

Passive voice

Traffic cases are decided by provincial court judges.

Passive voice can also depopulate sentences. No one appears to be taking any action in this sentence:

In provincial court, decisions on traffic cases come in on Thursdays.

There are times when you can use passive voice. In *The Transitive Vampire*, Karen Gordon writes:

When the person who did it or does it (whatever it is or was) is unknown or unimportant to the sense of the sentence, you may avail yourself of the passive voice.

When is the passive voice preferable?

In some situations, the passive voice is useful:

- If you want to put the emphasis on the receiver of the action, you can make it the subject:

    My client was severely injured as a result of your negligence.

- If the doer of the action is unimportant or unknown:

    This conclusion is based on a careful analysis of the case law.

- If you want to avoid mentioning the doer of the action:

    The decision was made without consulting the senior partners.

- If passive voice will let you maintain a consistent topic string in your paragraph:

    Jill testified that.... Jill's testimony is contradicted by John's guarantee of indebtedness.

- If passive voice allows you to keep your subject short:

    Active

    John's absolute and unconditional guarantee of Smith's mortgage and express promises to Chris contradict this testimony.

    Passive

    This testimony is contradicted by John's absolute and unconditional guarantee of Smith's mortgage and John's express promises to Chris.

- If you want to use a detached tone or express an abstraction:

    All people are created equal.

Loss of agency

The passive voice hides the roles and responsibilities of people. This produces a loss of agency and you don't know who is acting.

For example:

> *A confirmation of all searches is recommended. This is done by a search by mail request at the Bank of Canada.*

> *We recommend that you confirm all searches in writing. Request a search by mail from the Bank of Canada.*

Sometimes the passive voice is deliberately used to dehumanize a story. For example:

> *Thousands of civil service positions were cut in the last budget.*

The action is there but who is the actor? Who cut the jobs? Whose budget was it? Even the people who lost their jobs are hidden.

Cosmic detachment

The use of passive voice with nominalization reduces the human element in your writing, and has been described as cosmic detachment from issues and events.

Legal writing is often criticized for reducing the human element. When passive voice is combined with nominalizations, this results in cumulative loss of agency:

> *Elimination of thousands of civil service positions resulted from the last budget.*

Writing to control center stage

The reader of mystery novels has one question: *Who dunnit?*

When you use nominalizations and passive voice, you hide or disguise the actor and the action. The story becomes less immediate and direct. The most indirect writing eliminates the actor and uses abstract nouns with passive and impersonal phrases like "it seems" or "it appears".

Control the actors and the story by controlling the point of view.

When you are trying to make your client look better by disguising the client's role, you can use passives and nominalizations. Or, writing to your client to confess a colleague's blunder, you might say:

It seems the limitation date has passed.

When you chose to be ambiguous, choose the passive voice. It may even be courteous or diplomatic to do so. Sometimes, you dare not name the actor because it can cause embarrassment or serious repercussions.

You can control the story, and the reader's response, by your choice of active or passive verbs, hidden or key actors and clear or ambiguous words. Sometimes it will be in your client's interest to obscure the facts and the focus of responsibility. In this situation, you may want to use the style of avoidance and be indirect.

To be indirect, convert verbs to passive form, replace verbs with nominalizations, and eliminate actors. But remember, this style is not reader friendly.

There are times when you are not aiming for clarity and precision. Sometimes it is a matter of courtesy—it may be rude to state the obvious or identify the guilty party.

Breaking the rules

Some situations even justify violating the rules of grammar. If you are certain that it is necessary, go ahead. Situations where legal writer Timothy Perrin's "one unbreakable rule" demands application:

> *Occasionally, a good writer breaks rules for an effect. That's fine provided she knows what she is doing. So that is my only unbreakable rule. You can break any rule I tell you if*
>
> • *you know the rule*
>
> • *you know you are breaking it and*
>
> • *you can give a good reason why.*
>
> *Timothy Perrin, Better Writing for Lawyers*

Chapter Seven
Write Effective Sentences

Make the Sentences Easy

What kind of sentence is easiest for your reader? The problems with legal sentences are not always solved by keeping them short. The challenge is to make longer sentences understandable.

The first thing to do is check whether your sentences have these basic components that provide the core sentence:

- a noun or pronoun serving as the actor or **subject** of your sentence;
- a **verb** expressing the action taken by the subject;
- an **object**, if the verb requires it.

Here it is: The <u>client</u> <u>must pay</u> the <u>bill</u>
                     s   **v**   **o**

It is important to name the person or thing affected to complete your meaning. Is the person named or clearly implied? Who must do what to whom?

The client must pay the bill to the law firm.

Person affected

If the theme of the sentence is expressed through action that was done to the subject of the sentence, you are using passive voice. It is still important that the person or thing that took the action is named or apparent.

The bill was sent by the law firm's bookkeeper.

The bill was received by the accountant.

Follow normal subject-verb-object order

The usual English order of subject-verb-object for the parts of the sentence is easier for the reader to process than other constructions. Invert the order only when you want to stress the information at the end of the sentence.

For a basic sentence outline, answer these questions: *Who did What to Whom, How, When,* and *Where?*

Follow these guidelines:

- Keep the subject close to the verb or the verb close to the object
- Place modifiers and qualifiers outside the subject-verb-object order.
- Use lists and tabulation when they will help you structure the sentence.
- Avoid the habit of putting the subject at the opening of a long sentence and the verb at the end: that is legalese.

Here is a lawyer's sentence from a Letter to the Editor section of a newspaper. Notice the distance between the subject and its verb. The rewritten sentence below, now a paragraph, brings the core parts of that sentence together.

Traditional

The decision of Attorney-General to prefer an indictment against police Constable B. R. on a charge of attempted murder, after a judge, in a full and open hearing, found an entire absence of evidence on which to base such a charge, is utterly reprehensible.

Plainer

A judge, in a full and open hearing, dismissed a charge of attempted murder against police Constable B. R. The judge found there was no evidence on which to base the charge. The Attorney-General has now preferred a direct indictment against the constable on the same charge. This decision is utterly reprehensible.

See how the following sentence improves when the intervening phrase is taken out of the central core of the sentence:

Traditional

The Insurance Act provides that an insured (which is defined as the owner of the life insurance policy except in respect of group insurance, where it is defined as the group life insured) may in a contract or by declaration designate a beneficiary.

Plainer

The Insurance Act allows an insured to designate a beneficiary in a contract or by declaration. An "insured" is defined as the owner of the life insurance policy. In group insurance, the "insured" is the group.

The information embedded in the middle of the next sentence can be easily moved to another sentence:

Traditional

A claim, which in the case of negligent misconduct shall not exceed $500, and in the case of intentional misconduct shall not exceed $1,000, may be filed with the Criminal Injury Compensation Board by any injured party.

Plainer

Any injured party may file a claim with the Criminal Injury Compensation Board. A claim must not exceed $500 for negligent misconduct, or $1,000 for intentional misconduct.

Avoid legalese sentences

Legalese sentences don't work for clients. They are too long and are out of style. In fact the typical legalese sentence contains too many thoughts and tends to be grammatically faulty.

The following sentence is really three sentences jumbled together:

I hereby affirm that the above statements are true and correct and authorize the release to my employer of any information requested in respect of this claim and should I receive reimbursement for loss of wages or salary from any source other than my employer I will immediately notify my employer and agree to repay amounts in accordance with its employment policy.

Break them out.

Keep sentences short or simple

Sentences should generally contain only one thought. Long or complicated sentences create anxiety as the reader tries to break down and absorb the thoughts. They can be broken into shorter units by dissecting the different ideas. This sentence from a lawyer's letter is 63 words in length:

> *Because your letter goes on to state that you are seeking*
> *counsel and do not accept our statement of the legal*
> *consequences that can flow from your actions, I write on*
> *behalf of my client to demand again that you abandon your*
> *plans further to misuse my client's material and that you*
> *notify my client in writing that you agree to do so.*

Working memory extends to about 35 words for the more competent readers. A sentence longer than 35 words forces the reader to return to the beginning to read again to collate all the elements of the sentence.

For the average reader, the average sentence should be about 20 words, so structural simplicity is required. Putting qualifiers, modifiers and conditions into separate sentences, when possible, will help to keep sentences simple, and short. So the sentence above might read better as:

> *You say that you are seeking counsel since you disagree*
> *about the legal consequences that can flow from your*
> *actions. For my client I demand again that you abandon*
> *your plans to misuse my client's material. Please tell my*
> *client in writing that you agree to do so.*

Your intended meaning will surface if you divide complex thoughts into logical components:

Traditional

> *A person who acquired citizenship of the United States*
> *through birth abroad to a U.S. citizen parent or parents, but*
> *for whom an FS-240 was not completed, or a person who*
> *acquired U.S. citizenship by derivative naturalization, may*
> *apply for a CERTIFICATE OF CITIZENSHIP pursuant to*
> *the provisions of Section 341 of the Immigration and*
> *Nationality Act.*

Separate sentences and plainer language

Certain persons may apply for a Certificate of Citizenship under Section 341 of the Immigration and Nationality Act:

- *a person who was born abroad to a parent who was a U.S. citizen but whose birth was not registered through completion of an FS-240 form,*
- *a person who acquired U.S. citizenship by derivative naturalization (that is, after naturalization of the person's parent).*

Miscellaneous sentence problems

Avoid long or multiple introductory clauses before the main idea.

Legal writers use long introductory remarks before they express the main idea of the sentence. The exceptions and qualifications are set out before the principle.

This kind of sentence structure is not natural. It reverses the method used by the English language to deliver information. It is more effective to state the main idea, then bring in the secondary information in a separate clause or in a new sentence.

Traditional

If you change your occupation to one involving either a higher risk of accident or to one involving seasonal or casual employment, then we reserve the right to modify the terms which will apply to your Insurance while you are engaged in such occupation.

Plainer

We reserve the right to modify the terms of your Insurance if you change your occupation to one involving a higher risk of accident or to one involving seasonal or casual employment.

A common faux pas in legal writing is using a legal citation as the subject of a sentence:

Traditional

R. V. Collins, [1987] 1 S.C.R. 265 held that an accused must prove that his Charter rights or freedoms have been infringed or denied.

Plainer

The accused must prove that his Charter rights or freedoms have been infringed or denied. R.v. Collins, [1987] 1 S.C.R. 265 at 277.

Don't pack too much information in a sentence

Lawyers' sentences are usually too long and confused.

Complex sentence structures are sometimes necessary to express a complex idea. But complexity is different from complication. Complicated structures are never required. Check out the sentence below with 112 rambling words. A little more thought and a self-edit would have improved this lawyer's communication:

Similarly, if there has been physical cruelty by one spouse against the other but in spite of that the spouse who has been abused continues to remain in the marriage then the acts of cruelty that took place will be deemed to have been forgiven in a legal sense and can't be used to support the claim for divorce on the grounds of physical cruelty, although should there be a subsequent act of physical cruelty which, even though perhaps minor, was the straw that broke the camel's back, the previous acts of cruelty may be relevant to the claim for a divorce on the grounds of physical cruelty.

Adjectives, adverbs, and other phrases that modify or particularize words should be kept close to the words they affect. Longer modifiers and qualifiers should be kept out of the subject-verb-object connection. Here is a rewrite of the sentence above:

> *If physical cruelty occurs, but the abused spouse stays in the marriage:*
>
> - *the abused spouse is considered to have forgiven the other, and*
>
> - *there is no support for a divorce on grounds of physical cruelty.*
>
> *A later act of cruelty, if not forgiven, may revive the earlier acts to support a divorce on grounds of physical cruelty.*

Unstring the noun chains

Lawyers are prone to stringing together lists of nouns, with adjectives and adverbs interspersed. These complex noun strings are nouns used as adjectives to modify another noun. They are often not easy to understand. Here is a simple one: best drama actress winner Sally Field.

Consider these examples of noun chains:

> *cease and desist order compliance investigation reports*
>
> *voluntary professional self-regulation program assessment*
>
> *estate tax marital deduction provisions clause*

To fix noun chains, rewrite the idea or at least insert words to break up the chain. Use prepositions (of, by, to, about), verbs, and possessives in phrases modifying the last noun in the chain.

See how this sentence is clarified when it is revised to eliminate noun chains:

Chained

Registration of a Section 178 Bank Act Notice of Intention is a precondition to giving security.

Unchained

You must register a Notice of Intention as a precondition to taking security under Section 178 of the Bank Act.

Use Personal Perspectives

Use first or second person (*I* or *you*) point of view to avoid loss of agency and the detachment that can come from using the third-person perspective (*she, they, one*).

Traditional

The enclosed documents must be executed and returned to our offices.

Clearer

I have enclosed a release for you to sign and return to me.

You can also solve many of the problems of passive voice and loss of agency by using *I, we,* or *you.*

Traditional

As of today's date, the Social Service Tax Department, Bank of Canada, Employment Standards Branch and Personal Property Security Registry have advised that the Company is either not registered with them or that they have no outstanding assessments against the Company.

Plainer

We have searched the following registries and were informed on today's date that the Company is either not registered or does not owe outstanding assessments:

- Social Service Tax Department
- Bank of Canada
- Employment Standards Branch
- Personal Property Registry

If you already use first and second person perspective in your correspondence, consider using *you* more often—it sounds less self-important and more concerned with the reader.

Traditional

We have enclosed herewith the annual corporate minutes for Joe's Foods, Inc. for execution and return.

Plainer

You will find enclosed with this letter your annual corporate minutes for you to sign and return to me.

Use Tabulated Sentences and Lists

When information is complex or a sentence can't be shortened without reducing accuracy, break the sentence down into bits of information. The relationship between the bits of information can be expressed through the layout of the sentence. There are different patterns for the grammar and punctuation of tabulated sentences and lists.

Tabulated sentences are built like architectural blocks. The ideas are related and the sentence structure is built to show whether ideas are cumulative or comparative or opposing.

The next sentence is tabulated.

Meeting your mandatory CLE requirements requires

1) completing 12 hours of approved CLE credits

2) submitting proof of attendance

3) signing an affidavit certifying your attendance

4) submitting all paperwork to the proper registry

by February 1 of each year.

A sentence with a list is a simple sentence that includes a group of items. A paragraph can have a list of complete sentences.

Here follows an example.

The third presenter should answer the marketing questions:
- *What business topics are relevant and sought after?*
- *How can one get speaking requests like these?*
- *What does one do to follow up after a speaking engagement?*

Tabulated sentence structure

If necessary for clarity, use *and* or *or* before the last item. Using them will help the reader unravel a complicated passage, but even traditional legal writing allows you to use the conjunction only before the last item. Do not use them more than necessary, and do not use them if they are not needed for clarity.

If you are using a tabulated sentence in formal writing, the tabulated phrases must fit with the information in the introductory words and also with any closing words. Take special care in placing the closing words. In less formal documents, plain language style permits more leeway, as in the rewrite below.

The meaning of the following 46-word sentence is easier to grasp when the information is tabulated.

Traditional

Persons born abroad who are now 18 years of age or older and residing abroad and who may have a claim to U.S. citizenship, but have never been documented, should apply to the nearest American consular office for information and assistance in registering as U.S. citizens.

Tabulated, Plainer

A person born abroad who has never been documented as a U.S. citizen, who

- *is 18 years of age or older,*
- *resides abroad, and*
- *may have a claim to U.S. citizenship,*

should apply to the nearest American consular office for information and assistance to register as a U.S. citizen.

List structure

A list of similar items must be preceded by a complete sentence as it is in the next example.

The speaker will share common sense tips on how to improve communications with clients and colleagues:

- *the art of 'active' listening*
- *positive and negative communication*
- *the effect of non-verbal communication*
- *dealing with awkward or difficult issues*

Items in a list are not functional parts of the sentence. Each item is self-contained and independent, and if a full sentence, can be capitalized and punctuated with a period. If the items are neither cumulative nor alternative, there is no need for *and* or *or*.

Maintain Parallel Structures

Parallelism refers to using the same grammatical form for each item in a list whether it consists of phrases, clauses or sentences. Putting the items in parallel form can also clarify their meaning.

Parallel sentence form

Your memorandum has good structure, was well researched, and should answer their questions.

The writer of the following sentence might have avoided grammatical error by using parallelism:

The effective date of the search will be the close of business on the date requested and will be available for pickup after 9:30 a.m. the next day, or can be mailed directly to the law firm.

Parallel items in tabulated sentence

The search will be

- *effective as of close of business on the date of request*
- *available for pick up the following morning after 9:30*
- *mailed to your firm on request*

provided that you have sufficient credit in your account.

In lists and tabulated sentences, the presence or absence of parallelism is more apparent than in regular prose.

List with parallel form

Retainer Agreement

Services under this agreement

On behalf of the estate, I will:

- *prepare all documents needed to obtain a grant*
- *file probate documents with the court*

- *confirm title and registration of assets*
- *transfer the assets to your name as executor and then to the beneficiaries.*

Layout of lists and tabulations

Lists can make text as easy to read as numbered tables. Lists are a visual way of presenting information. Review your draft to check if there are any lists embedded in the text.

Lists should include no more than seven items—people are able to process or remember groups of three to five items better than they do longer lists.

Do not use a numbering system unless the items are chronological, prioritized, or of different value in some respect.

Items in a list must be

- similar in nature
- parallel in form
- equal in importance.

Use these formats to set material apart from regular text:

spacing—*to establish a separate unit,*

indentation —*on the left only or on both left and right,*

double column format—*for long lists of short items,*

numerical or alphabetic listing—*to rank items,*

special characters *where there is no ranking:*

- *bullets for short lists of short phrases,*

– *dashes for longer lists of sentences or paragraphs,*

□ *boxes for checklists or when ticking boxes is necessary.*

Chapter Eight
Design Paragraphs That Work

Paragraphs Have Logic

Paragraph development is an art that is easy to learn. These are basic guidelines:

- Keep paragraphs short.
- Develop only one topic per paragraph.
- Link sentences in a paragraph.
- Use transition words properly.

A paragraph brings together sentences about a topic. Use a topic sentence to focus your ideas or arguments on the topic. You can start a paragraph with a topic sentence if it is convenient to do so.

It is not necessary to create a special legal method for paragraphing. Lawyers sometimes refer to individual items in lists or tabulations as paragraphs but it is a mistake to think this way generally. A single sentence or a phrase in a table or list does not make a paragraph just because it is in a table or list.

A sculptured paragraph like that becomes a real paragraph only when it is composed of a series of complete sentences like the first paragraph above.

Cover One Topic

A paragraph is usually made up of two parts: a topic sentence, and other sentences that support or elaborate the topic. The topic sentence gives the main idea; the other sentences can further define, describe, or detail the topic.

How do you develop the topic in a paragraph? By analogy, contrast, example, chronology, definition, comparison, or evidence.

If the other sentences introduce new ideas instead of elaborating the topic, then those sentences deserve new paragraphs.

Keep Paragraphs Short

Introduce only one topic in a paragraph to keep it short.

For reading by clients and the public, a paragraph should be between two and five lines of text — for the modern reader this is more important than the number of sentences.

You can scan a document quickly to check for long or dense paragraphs, then decide whether or not to break them up or restructure them.

If you must write a longer paragraph, be sure to keep the sentences to an average length of 20 words each. Break out a long paragraph into lists and tabulations.

Most grammarians advise against paragraphs containing only one sentence. A one-sentence paragraph is justified only if the sentence is complicated or if it is used for emphasis.

Link the Sentences

Topic strings

Start the paragraph by stating the topic and pick a keyword or phrase in this topic sentence. Every sentence that follows can have your chosen keyword or phrase, or a synonym or pronoun for the keyword. In this way, each sentence in the paragraph refers to the central idea, creating a topic string that ties the sentences together.

Keywords

To hold a paragraph together, you can create a linking chain of keywords. Pick a keyword from your first sentence. Start the second sentence with the keyword or a synonym for it. Pick another keyword from the second sentence and use it to start the third sentence, and so on.

The keywords or phrases serve as links between the sentences. They are used to construct a paragraph. Do not confuse keywords with elegant variation, as Henry Watson Fowler put it in Modern English Usage in 1926. Elegant variation is the unnecessary use of synonyms to display your wealth of vocabulary, when a single word works just fine.

Don't use synonyms that will cause confusion over important information. It is better to keep calling a banana a banana than to cause confusion or seek a tortured substitute such as "a curved, elongated yellow fruit."

Use the same word throughout the document to avoid confusion.

Use transition words

You can use transition words to emphasize the relationship or development of ideas within a paragraph.

Examples of transition words are: *however, moreover, similarly, conversely, yet,* and *while.* But don't rely on these words to make the relationships between ideas apparent–transition words can only serve to provide links for sentences in the paragraph.

Beware of using too many contrast words for transition as they will result in the same mental gymnastics as multiple negatives. Contrast words include: *conversely* and *alternately.* Try for something plainer like *but, instead,* or *yet.*

Move from old information to new information in sequence. This puts emphasis on the new or important information.

Sometimes you will use a whole sentence as a transition to warn the reader of a sudden change of direction. When you change the subject, actor, time, place, or perspective, a transition word or sentence serves as a signpost.

Example of transition sentences:

> *That closes the discussion of the wrongful dismissal of Mr. Jones. We turn now to consider the question of the libelous statements made about him by the employer.*

Part 3
Practical applications

Legal Writing Formats

Legal writing has some special forms, constraints, and requirements.

In this part, you will learn about those used every day: memorandums, letters, and opinions. These formats are adaptable enough to allow you to follow the guidelines discussed earlier about organizing your information for your reader.

Legal drafting refers to legal writing of contracts and other documents which create or record rights and obligations between people. Special rules for legal drafting are not covered in this work.

Persuasive writing is needed in litigation documents. Special techniques for persuasive writing and general formats for litigation are not covered in this manual. Yet I can assure you that plain language is more persuasive than other writing styles!

Guidelines and Resources

Most writers in law offices stumble along without the most basic resources. There is no need for that. Chapter Ten provides guidelines for visual presentation through document design and page layout. The final chapter tells you what sources of help you can keep at hand. And the Internet links included throughout provide access to more reading material.

Chapter Nine
Modern Legal Correspondence

Modern communication technology provides speed and efficiency, but it can't write an effective business letter for you. You need plain language techniques to get your message through efficiently and effectively.

Each piece of legal correspondence requires fresh thought and effort, even when you revise a standard-form letter. The communication speed available through fax and email does not excuse you from the application of thought and analysis to your letters.

Your letters, more than any other piece of writing, express your style and personality. They will influence your client's perception of you.

Write in a tone and style similar to the way you speak; don't undergo a Jekyll and Hyde transformation when you set about writing legal correspondence. Tone is very important in to keeping clients satisfied with your services.

This chapter provides a checklist for better writing, and details topics in this checklist:

1. Clarify your purpose.

2. Consider your reader.

3. Write complete and accurate business letters.

4. Organize the letter for highest impact.

5. Choose your words thoughtfully.

6. Use modern formats.

7. Keep the psychology of readers in mind.

Clarify Your Purpose

When beginning a writing task, you first need to settle on your exact purpose for writing, then focus on your reader. Of course, you also need to know your subject well. These three factors will control the content, tone, and style of your letter.

Legal letters are specialized business letters. You write business letters to

- question
- inform
- persuade
- acknowledge facts
- record processes
- record agreements

Consider Your Reader

Once you are clear about your purpose, your next step is to determine your reader's concerns. Put yourself in the reader's place and figure out how you'd want to be addressed in that situation. The skills, interests, vocabulary, and knowledge level of your reader will determine your tone (generally professional but considerate), vocabulary (familiar), and the amount of detail and explanation required.

Traditional Language

The statement for professional services which you will find enclosed herewith is, in all likelihood, somewhat in excess of your expectations. In the circumstances, I believe it is appropriate for me to avail myself of this opportunity to provide you with an explanation of the causes therefor.

Plain Language

The bill I am sending you with this letter is probably higher than you expected, and I would like to explain why.

Traditional Language

This is to acknowledge your letter of recent date, the contents of which have been duly noted. In the third paragraph thereof...

Plain Language

I have received and carefully considered your letter of June 13. In its third paragraph...

Show respect for your reader

If you are writing to your own client, be considerate about the client's state of mind, knowledge of the area of law, familiarity with legal terminology, and level of interest in the legal issues.

To earn the reader's full attention:

- Write to the correct person.
- Get that person's name and position right.
- Use an appropriate salutation and closing.
- Be consistent with earlier correspondence to the same person.
- Be courteous and diplomatic.
- Use non-sexist language.
- Adjust your tone to suit the reader's sensibilities.

Write Complete and Accurate Letters

The content and format of your letter will depend on your purpose and the reader's interests. Each letter you write should be complete in itself. Your reader should not have to read a legal file to understand your letter; if they must, it will result in delays.

Use file reference numbers

Use both your own and the reader's file reference numbers. File reference numbers help because you or the reader (a senior lawyer, for example) may represent the client in more than one legal matter. In a large firm, you may even have two clients with the same name.

Give a clear notice

Use the subject line to identify your client, the reader's client, and the specific reason for writing. The subject or reference line should also include a mention of the specific topic of the letter, for example, "Smith v. Harvey - Scheduling of Discoveries", is better than a general reference to "Smith v. Harvey - Personal Injury Matter".

Simplify your reference line

Modernize the style of the reference line. You don't need to include Re: or Subject: in your reference line. The reference line is conceptually part of the body of the letter and should be closer to it than to the address. Use bold type, italics, capitals or underline to highlight the subject line, but don't combine techniques.

Introduce yourself and your topic

Your opening paragraph should introduce you or your purpose in writing. This provides a context for the issue being discussed. Be specific enough to catch the reader's attention, and don't repeat information stated in the reference line.

It is usually not necessary to identify the last letter you received from your correspondent. When you are responding to a specific settlement offer or statement of terms, however, it does become necessary to identify previous correspondence because you want to make clear what you are agreeing with.

Identify the letter you are answering by its date or summarize its contents.

Example:

I am writing to accept the terms of settlement proposed by you in a letter dated April 16, 1996.

With letters being sent electronically, it may not be enough to identify the letter by date alone. You may need to state the gist of the letter to which you are replying:

We write to clarify the terms of settlement proposed in our May 15 letter, which you appeared to accept by way of a restatement of the terms in a letter also dated May 15, 1996. Our client has not offered to...

If there has been much delay between receiving a letter and sending a reply, it helps to summarize the letter to which you are responding. If necessary, you can itemize the points agreed to at a later point in the letter.

In April, you wrote proposing that the Delaney Estate might be brought to an early conclusion by means of an agreement between the potential beneficiaries to a compromise. We can now respond to your suggestions....

Fully set out all the relevant facts

Give the reader all the information needed to deal with your letter. If information is missing, the reader must obtain the client file in order to review earlier letters and reports, telephone messages and so on. If your letter is complete in itself, the reader is likely to respond sooner.

If you are replying to an earlier letter, show how the new information you are providing relates back to that letter. You can refer to the questions you are answering:

You ask whether our client has obtained an estimate....

You question why the employer should be responsible for...

Answer the questions:
Who, What, When, Where, Why, And How?

Sometimes the best way to organize your letter is to answer the "Five W" questions: *who, what, when, where* and *why. How* is often added as a sixth. These are the questions that journalists are trained to answer.

If you consider all these questions, you will probably produce a more complete letter than you would otherwise. This method works particularly well when your letter is the first letter in the matter. After you have described what is to be done, be sure to explain how. Make certain that you have made it clear who is to do what.

> We will now _____. When we have had your reply, we can then _____.

> We assume that you will proceed to _____. All that will then remain is for us to _____.

Close with care

The closing paragraph should not be a stock phrase but a genuine expression of courtesy. Choose your tone carefully: The final words of your letter will echo in the reader's mind and leave a general impression.

Stay away from trite phrases like these:

> *Thank you in advance for...*

> *We look forward to hearing from you at your earliest convenience...*

> *Hoping for the favor of an early reply...*

Give a call to action

In closing, give a call to action to focus the reader on what you expect next. Restate briefly what you want or expect the reader to do. Or indicate what course of action you are going to take next.

Try a direct specific statement:

> *Promptly after hearing from you, we will...*

Use a courteous request or instruction:

Will you please notify us when...

Please mail the signed release to...

Close with a question:

Please let us know when it will be convenient for you to...

Considering all this, should we revoke the offer?

Organize the Letter for Highest Impact

Organize by topic.

Put the topics in an order that suits your audience and purpose.

Keep paragraphs short.

If your letter is long, use the second paragraph as a prose table of contents:

> *In this letter, I'll explain the incorporation documents that are enclosed. I'll review the organizing resolutions of the company. Then I'll discuss the annual duties of the secretary of the company to look after its legal affairs.*

Use topic headings to break up a long letter.

Use tabulation and lists whenever possible to break up the dense text in a long letter.

Keep forms parallel.

Use parallel forms of grammar for ideas of equivalent impact or application.

Use a cover letter.

Many overly long letters can be converted to a short cover letter with a number of schedules or lists attached.

Lawyers often ask that a duplicate copy of a letter be signed and returned to confirm the client's agreement to a retainer or terms of settlement. It is preferable to write a cover letter explaining what you are doing and enclosing two copies of a letter of agreement, with one to be signed and returned.

Choose Your Words Thoughtfully

Use everyday words

The simpler your words, the clearer your message. There is no excuse for using legal jargon in letters to clients or business associates. If you must use legal terms of art then provide a brief explanation or definition and apply it to the circumstances.

Avoid jargon, wordiness and repetition

Ensure, indemnify, and *save harmless* have similar or overlapping meanings. Your client will not understand these words or the distinctions between them. Try to express your meaning in the simple, clear language that you might use to explain the term to your client orally.

One word that is widely used in situations where it is unnecessary is *execution*. *To execute* is to do what is necessary to make a document valid, and this can include these four steps: 1. signing, 2. sealing, 3. delivering, and 4. carrying out performance of the obligations. When you want a client to come to your office to sign a document, say just that—don't ask the client to execute anything unless you mean something more.

Use ordinary, familiar words

Everyone, even a business professional, appreciates language that is easy to understand.

When you write to other lawyers, you know that the letter will also be read by a layperson—either your client or the other lawyer's client, so don't write in legalese. Remember Benson's definition of a necessary term of art:

> *A genuine, technical, term of art has an uncontroversial core meaning that cannot be conveyed succinctly in any other way.*

Trite phrases

Drop the old clichés and clusters of unnecessary words: write as you would speak in professional settings. Those formalisms that make legal correspondence stuffy have to go.

Cross-out phrases like these:

> *We are in receipt of...*
>
> *This is to acknowledge your letter...*
>
> *Confirming our telephone conversation...*
>
> *This is in reply to your letter of...*
>
> *It is important to add that...*
>
> *In this regard, it is of significance that...*
>
> *It is interesting to point out that...*
>
> *I should further point out...*
>
> *It is my considered opinion...*
>
> *Let me take this opportunity to...*

Try these substitutes:

Traditional Language	*Plain Language*
at this point in time	*now*
in the event of	*if*

pursuant to the terms of	*under*
under date of	*on, dated*
meets with our approval	*We approve*
move for a continuance	*ask the court to postpone*
Attached please find	*Attached is*
I am of the opinion that	*I think*
I am not in a position to	*I cannot*
In compliance with	
your request	*As you asked*

Watch your tone

What tone should you adopt? It really depends on what is appropriate to your purpose, or what your correspondence is trying to accomplish.

Be no more formal than necessary—there is a tendency amongst lawyers to adopt a pompous tone that, far from impressing the reader, is alienating. As Henry Weihofen advised: "aim for the simplicity and buoyancy of good conversation."

The letter that follows does not adopt an appropriate tone. It is from a lawyer to a legal research consultant (with no introduction and no previous discussion of this subject):

Dear Sirs:

Please find enclosed herewith a list of publications that are required by the writer. Please advise the writer if any of the enclosed publications are available to you and/or the writer and if so, how do we go about obtaining them?

Your prompt attention to this matter is greatly appreciated,

Use Modern Formats

If your firm does not have a required style, the block letter form is modern and efficient. Do not justify text at the right margin and do keep the date, headings, and signature lines aligned at the left margin.

Legal correspondence is top-heavy.

Take a look at the first page of some letters and you see no room for text. The letterhead takes up a major chunk of space, the full address needs a few lines, and, of course, several lines are devoted to codes about method of delivery, file reference numbers, date, attention lines, salutation, subject lines, and so on.

Often a one-page letter is forced to stretch to two pages just to accommodate such information and the complementary close and signature lines.

Modern business formats condense the space required by eliminating the salutation and closing. Legal correspondents who adopted this practice report no one has ever commented on their absence.

Salutations

Putting aside such traditional problems as needing to know the sex of the addressee and her marital status if it's a woman, salutations continue to pose problems. When writing to another firm or to an organization, you often do not know who will be the recipient of the letter. And sometimes keeping the salutation and closing complementary is a task in itself.

Eliminate the salutation

The solution is to skip the salutation. If you don't know the individual's name and you are writing to the holder of a particular job, use the position title, placing it directly above the address:

Managing Partner
Litigation Department
Holmes, Henrik and Hoben
456 Suisse Place
Zurich, Switzerland

When you are using an attention line to identify an individual, don't use a salutation. A salutation is repetitious here anyway:

Smith, Hobkirk and Smitt
124 Horten Boulevard
Denton, Alberta A3T 1W3
Attention: Ms. Doris Elton
Corporate Legal Assistant

When you don't use a salutation, you don't need to use a complementary close, unless it seems more polite to do so. *Complementary* means here: to complete the whole. The salutation and the complementary closing ought to be like matching book ends: both the salutation and the closing should be similar in tone and formality.

Choose a neutral form

If you know a woman's name, you can include it in the attention line without referring to marital status:

Attention: Barbara Ward, Personnel Administrator

Or you can use her full name in the salutation: "Dear Barbara Ward," or use *Ms.*—created for just this purpose.

Instead of the "Dear Sirs," use "Ladies and Gentlemen," or use the name of the department: "Dear Litigation Department,".

Once you've begun corresponding with someone, adopt their chosen position title and any other designation. It is a good idea to put a question on your client-intake form to find out the client's preferred form of address.

Parallelism in closing phrases

Keep your salutation and closing parallel and harmonious.

The closing phrase in a letter is called the complementary close because it is supposed to be parallel in tone and style with the salutation. Here are some parallel pairs:

Most formal tone
  Sir or Madam: Yours respectfully,
  Madam: Respectfully,
The judicial formal
  The Honorable Allan Harney
  Chief Justice of British Columbia
  Dear Chief Justice Harney: Yours respectfully,
Formal tone
  Dear Ms. Sampson: Very truly yours,
  Dear Sir or Madam: Yours truly,
Business-like tone
  Dear Mr. Thompson, Yours sincerely,
  Dear Miss Smith, Sincerely,
Familiar tone
  Dear Mallory, Most sincerely,
  Dear Tom Johnson, Best regards,

Psychology for Good News or Bad News

Set the scene to make the reader comfortable

The structure of a letter sometimes causes information anxiety in the reader. You can help the reader focus on your message by setting up the scene in your introductory paragraph itself. Then isolate points of difference, and identify areas of agreement. This way you narrow the actual issues in dispute and avoid an argumentative tone.

Many clients or lawyers (reading other lawyers' letters) have learned to flip to the last page of a document. They know that they will find the answers to their questions and the context for the letter in the final paragraph or two. Then they go back and read the letter from the beginning to get the detail or follow the argument. Well-organized documents don't require this.

At the beginning, fix the questions in the reader's mind as a framework for the rest of the letter. A brief version of your answer or conclusion always goes in the beginning. The body of the letter explains how you reached your conclusion.

Give positive news early

If you have something positive to report, don't keep the reader in suspense. A long introduction produces apprehension. Say "yes" quickly, then supply the necessary details and close your letter in a friendly or upbeat way.

Give bad news in a neutral or positive tone

Remember that nobody likes rejection. A letter that says "no" is best written in a neutral or constructive tone. At least say thank you for the request, complaint, or offer.

Speaking in the first person will give your remarks a human touch. Try to be understanding and sympathetic. Be careful to reject the request, not the person who made it. Begin neutrally with something that lets you get easily into the subject.

Ideas for tone

- Find something important you can agree on.
- Concede what you can't win.
- If you have made a mistake, admit it.

When you are reporting a decision you have made, set out the context for your decision so the reader is receptive. If you are able to disclose the reasons, explain why you rejected the request.

Be gracious when you deliver the unwelcome message. Try to say "no" indirectly rather than directly. Let the reader infer the "no".

Provide an out for the recipient—suggest a positive alternative to what he or she originally sought, or some other solution to the problem. Close with a positive statement, even if it is only an offer to consider any future requests.

How to say *No*

Even if your message is negative, try to keep "no" letters positive or matter-of-fact in tone. Speak in the first person and add the human touch. Reject the request, not the person who made it.

1. Say thank you for the request.

2. State the context for the decision so you can prepare the reader.

Unfortunately, the courts have not addressed this question before...

3. Say "no" graciously (or by inference).

To take this case would be to mislead you as to the likelihood of eventual success...

4. Provide an out (a positive alternative).

If other supportive facts come to light, do not hesitate to contact me again.

5. Close with a positive statement.

I appreciate your consulting me about this matter and would be pleased to discuss other matters with you in future.

Chapter Ten
Legal Memorandums and
Letter Opinions

Robert B. Smith described the purpose and content of a legal memorandum:

> *The memorandum is written in a law office. The writer takes a client's problem based on a set of real facts, discovers the applicable law, applies that law to the facts, assesses the client's chance of success, and, usually, recommends a course of action. The memo is complete within itself; another lawyer need read only the memo itself to understand the matter and make decisions about it.*
>
> *The Literate Lawyer: Legal Writing & Oral Advocacy*

The Memorandum versus the Opinion

The legal memorandum is usually prepared not for the client but for another lawyer in the firm. It may serve as the first draft in the preparation of a letter of opinion to the client.

Audience

The audience and purpose for the memorandum is different from the audience and purpose for a letter of opinion. So you must do more than condense the memorandum into a letter.

You need to reconsider the organization of the document, the word choices, and whether it is necessary to include references to legislation or cases. Since other lawyers will read your legal memorandums, while your letter opinions are directed to your clients, who may even publish them, all the original choices have to be reconsidered.

In drafting a contract, you need to anticipate future developments, something you don't have to do in such detail in a letter of opinion — your client usually wants to know only what applies in the particular circumstances at the present time. The client would only be confused reading many qualifications and exceptions.

You have to use your judgement to decide which exception should concern the client because it might come into play. But don't let remote possibilities dominate the communication of the facts and the main proposition.

Purpose

In writing letters of opinion, your primary purpose is to advise your client on rights, remedies, or liabilities. Your secondary purpose may be to advise the client on alternative courses of action where the proposed course of action is not lawful.

The client may have his or her own purpose in seeking the opinion, which is something you should bear in mind when determining your writing approach. They may want to quote your opinion to a rival, or use it in support of their own position with a board of directors, or release it to the press (or quote it in a press release) to justify their position.

In a legal memorandum, you may have to set out minor facts or cases to let the senior lawyer in your firm know that you have considered them. You may want to let the senior lawyer assess their applicability, but, again, they should not be included in a letter to the client unless clearly relevant to your conclusions.

Only new legislation or new, precedent-setting cases should be named or quoted to clients.

Follow this advice from Richard D. Lee:

> "Address the client's concerns. Too often opinion letters describe the attorney's journey through the library rather than focus on the client's questions. The client is rarely interested in your research.
>
> Address the client's questions. The client asks, what should I do? To which the lawyer too often responds, here is the law!
>
> Consider the client. You are writing to a real person or group of people. Too often legal opinions are cold and impersonal. Instead, construct your opinion to put your client at ease, satisfied that you are addressing the client directly. Your opinion should show that you care about your client and his or her problems."
>
> Legal Opinions: Style, Structure, and Organization, Law Society of Upper Canada CLE Materials

The Writing Process and Purpose

Purpose

To be clear about your purpose, you need to have a clear idea of where you are headed. An important step in preparing a legal memorandum, or memorandum of law as it is also called, is getting proper direction about its purpose.

If you have received only vague directions, as often happens, you may need to take the initiative to have the instructions clarified or amplified so the purpose is clear.

Determine whether the memorandum is needed to:

- decide whether to take a case,
- advise a client,
- draft a pleading,
- persuade someone,
- prepare for trial.

Organization

The organization, format, and style you choose for your document should arise from your determination of the purpose and the likely readers. The primary consideration in organization for both the reader and the purpose is utility. What organizing system will work best and most efficiently?

If the conclusion you have reached is negative or disappointing to the client, you may want to organize a letter of opinion in the format suggested for delivering bad news in letters in the previous chapter.

General Style Matters

Modern formats

Modern conventions for organization and format for memorandums or opinions exist, although there are alternative approaches (many firms have their own styles). The formats suggested here are common.

Each format is described on a separate page and then a comparison is provided below. There is general discussion of style and format.

Verb tense

Most guidelines suggest that you state

- Facts and court decisions in the past tense.
- Legal rules in the present tense.
- Recommendations in future tense.

Word choices

In a letter of opinion, you express your considered conclusion based on logic and reason, so the following phrases expressing feelings, beliefs, and inclination are not appropriate:

I believe ... I feel ...

I suppose ... I am leaning toward ...

If you don't know something, say so. If you haven't figured something out, say you are still investigating. State clearly that you are speculating on a given set of assumptions, or that you need to further investigate facts before you can form a certain opinion. Use introductory comments like this:

Reason suggests...   I hold the opinion that...

The authorities conclude...   I recommend...

I suggest taking the approach that...

Statute references

Most firms have adopted a particular style for references to statutes.

You may need to quote portions of a statute, regulation, article, transcript, or other material. If you want to quote more of the statute for better context, put it in an appendix. Your reader will appreciate being provided the full text of an item such as a city by-law, which may not be readily available in the law office or business office.

Citations

There are some legalisms you cannot avoid—case citations, for example. But do not cite cases in letters of opinion unless the client is familiar with the case law (for example, accountants with tax cases) or unless the case is groundbreaking.

In legal memorandums, do not let citations interfere with your message. Remember to avoid long introductory phrases in your sentences. It is better to let the citation stand alone at the end of a sentence or paragraph. Statements like this make it difficult for the reader to grasp the point, when it finally arrives:

> *In Norton v. Commander, 1999 (89) ALT 34 at 36, 1999 34 WER 684 at 687, the Court held...*

Instead of following that style, state the important conclusion from the case, then append the citation.

> *The law is clear that... See Norton v. Commander, 1999 (89)...*

Avoid string citations

Cite only the leading case in the text of your letter or memorandum. If you need to cite three or four other cases, put the citations in a footnote. Or use endnotes at the back of your memorandum or use a schedule.

No one reads a long string of citations, especially if it is italicized or underlined. The eye just skips over text blocks with such features. String citations also pose a problem to the reader in connecting the introductory words with the ideas that follow the list.

Footnotes

Excessive use of footnotes is a common offence among legal writers. Anything that is essential to understanding the text should be in the text itself, not in footnote. In letter opinions, there should be no footnotes.

For authority on this point, see "Lost Words: The Economical, Ethical and Professional Effects of Bad Legal Writing," Occasional Papers 7, Section of Legal Education and Admissions to the Bar, American Bar Association, Indianapolis, 1994.

Quotations

Legal writers use too many quotations. Don't quote someone else unless the way the writer has expressed the thought is a gem you cannot equal. When referring to case precedents, summarize or paraphrase whenever you can. When you must quote, be precise in selecting what must be used and what can be cut.

Form and Layout

Signposts

Other chapters offered general guidelines on how to use titles, headings, and other aspects of form and layout. These are specific suggestions for memorandums and opinions.

Use keywords in headings and titles to make it easier for those who will be filing or indexing the legal memorandums in your office. A title or heading that poses the question the memorandum answers will be helpful to future researchers.

Any document longer than three pages needs a table of contents. In shorter documents, you could provide a prose version of the table of contents at the beginning.

Patterns of Persuasion

When you want to be persuasive, you may choose to use a specific pattern of organization that suits that purpose.

Persuasive documents are written with the purpose of proving that a conclusion is sound or a recommendation ought to be put into effect. Try this variation on the ancient Greek and Roman style of argument:

Overview statement

Positive statement of position

Statement of facts

Statement of organization of contents

Confirmation of supportive facts

Examination of contrary facts

Discussion: weighing the facts, assessing both sides of the argument

Conclusion and call to action

Application of a New Theory

This approach is to be used in letters or arguments when an entirely new theory is applied to the law or facts.

A core body of legal principles and cases is well known to lawyers and the courts, because it is referred to so frequently, and because each practitioner or judge in that field of law is intimately familiar with it. You do not need to elaborate the basic principles of existing law when you are advocating for a new approach.

So start with the new theory, but remember to recap it in conclusion. The last impression you leave must be your interpretation of law as applied to the particular facts.

Introduction and overview

Description of theory

a. describe it

b. establish its validity

c. defend its use in this case

Statement of facts

Discussion and interpretation of facts according to theory

Briefly apply and interpret theory

Refute contrary facts and dispute older theory

Recap of application of your new theory

Conclusion and recommendation

Another approach

An alternative model is designed for use when readers may not be familiar with the existing law and its underlying theory.

Introduction

Brief explanation of competing theories

Statement of facts

Discussion and confutation of older theory as applied to facts

New theory

- *describe it*
- *establish its validity*
- *defend its use in this case*

Interpretation of the data according to the theory

Implications of the interpretation

Conclusion with recommendation

Legal Memorandum Structure

Heading and introduction

Identify the client and how or why the matter or research assignment was referred to you.

Issues

Set out the basic legal questions that you will answer.

Summary

Provide a brief answer to the questions. Brief here means no more than five to ten lines.

Statement of facts

Set out all the important facts. If there is a dispute over the facts, set out both versions. Be as brief as possible. You can set the facts out chronologically or by another method. (See Chapter Three on organization.) Inadequate statements of facts are the major problem with legal memorandums.

Survey of pertinent statutes

While this section is optional, your reader will find it helpful to have the applicable statutory provisions set out. If the provisions are long, paraphrase them here, and set them out on an attachment.

Survey of precedents

You must review the relevant, primary precedents governing the facts. It is usually not necessary to prepare a history of the case law; the most recent or definitive cases will suffice.

Discussion of each issue

A dispassionate discussion of the issues and the applicable law is the central purpose of the memorandum. In this section you predict the answers that a court would give if it were faced with your facts, given the pertinent law.

Conclusion

This is a summary of your predictions about the state of the law and its application to your case. This is where you expand on the brief answer furnished at the beginning.

Recommendation

You recommend the best solution to the problem facing the client. What should the client do? What do you propose to do for the client? These are the questions you answer here.

Legal Opinion Structure

Heading and introduction

Identify the client's problem and how the matter came to you.

Statement of legal issues raised

Pose the question the client needs answered. Rephrase the question that was put to you by the client in a way that the law can provide an answer, or reformulate the question as a result of your analysis of the real issue.

Brief answer

Give the shortest possible answer to the question posed, or advise the client what must or must not be done:

> *You are entitled to _____, because....*
>
> *Yes, you may _____. However, you cannot _____...*
>
> *You cannot _____, but you could consider _____...*

Statement of facts on which the opinion is based

Set out the relevant facts. If you or your client is not aware of all the facts, set out the assumptions you have made.

Include a warning that the facts and assumptions set out were considered in the state of the law prevailing on the date of the opinion.

Discussion of how you reached the conclusion

Give your explanation or documentation of the logic and the law, from the client's perspective if possible.

Restatement and elaboration of conclusion

Provide a fuller explanation of your brief answer at the beginning. If your conclusion is negative, or will disappoint or annoy your client, you may want to lead up to it gradually and save the answer until this point in your letter. It may also help to explain the policy behind the law that is having the negative effect on your client.

Recommendations and proposals for action

Suggest what the client should do, or what you will do for the client once you receive instructions. If your conclusion was negative, you can offer alternative courses of action here. If you recommend that the client send a letter to someone to make a demand or a proposal, either provide a draft letter, or suggest the relevant wording and request that you see the client's letter before it is sent.

Summary: Which format?

Memo	Opinion	Persuasion	New Theory
Intro & overview	Overview	Overview	Overview
Legal issues	Legal issues	Positive position	Description of theory
Summary	Short answer	Organization of contents	
Statement of facts	Facts		Statement of facts
Survey of pertinent statutes, precedents	Discussion	Statement of facts	Discussion and interpretation
	Conclusion	Confirmation of supportive facts	
Discussion	Recommendation		Apply & interpret theory
Conclusion		Examination of contrary facts	
Recommendation			Confutation of older theory
		Discussion of your position applied to facts	
			Recap of new theory
		Conclusion	
			Conclusion and Recommendation
		Call to action	

Chapter Eleven
Guidelines for Visual
Presentation

The public prefers to read material that looks easy to read and interesting. Good design encourages people to pay attention to what you have to say.

Good page design strengthens the text and shows connections between ideas. When you need to reach the 48% of Canadians with reading problems a simple layout is necessary and graphics both complement and supplement the written text.

Consider plain language and design issues when you design your office letterhead.

The four main principles of good page design are

- simplicity
- contrast
- organization
- image

Simplicity

Remove clutter

You need to reduce the visual clutter competing for readers' attention. Don't take advantage of every design feature available from your desktop publishing program. And don't use features that fragment the page. Aim to unify it.

Use restraint

Use as few lines and boxes as possible. Practice restraint with tinted backgrounds and reverse type. Minimize your use of underlining.

Contrast

Creating visual contrast prevents gray pages that look to the reader like a mass of type without an attractive starting point.

Make your headlines and subheads stand out and draw the reader's attention to the text. Use larger type, a different typeface, surrounding white space, or bold type.

Use open space

Use white space and openness to make reading look easy. To avoid the look of cramped, dense text, use shorter paragraphs, use subheads and indentations, and indent lists of items.

Use color for contrast

Colored print or paper makes your material more attractive. Pale yellow or cream offers good contrast to black type without glare. Green print works well on white or off-white paper.

Only use bright colors in headlines or graphics. But consider using your yellow highlighter to emphasize important headings or key words in outgoing correspondence.

Typeface and type size

Type size describes the height and width of type characters.

The fine print in legal documents is usually 8 point or smaller. Most people are comfortable reading type that is 10 point or larger. People over 40 years need a larger type size—at least 10 to 12 point, depending on the typeface used.

White space or negative space

The white space framing and flowing through text can be used to good effect. Margins—left and right, top and bottom—should be at least one inch wide. Wider side margins are recommended for ease in reading and note taking.

Within the text, white space can be produced by

- having short paragraphs,
- varying the size of paragraphs,
- using subheads,
- using indentation,
- making indented lists.

White space promotes readability, but avoid the look of wasting space. Consolidate white space rather than sprinkle it over the page. Don't become so preoccupied with the white space that you lose sight of more substantive concerns.

Capitals or lower case?

Lower case type helps the reader to recognize the words on the page.

Words in lower case have distinct shapes that are recognizable—lower case letters have ascenders and descenders, heads and tails, which make them distinguishable from one another.

Capital letters should only be used to begin sentences and proper names. Think twice about any other uses. Don't capitalize whole words as headings, or for emphasis. The old legal practice of using a string of capitalized words to indicate a new paragraph is no longer needed now that indentation, bold type, and double-spacing between paragraphs are being used.

Text line length

The best length for a line of text is one that is most comfortable on the reader's eye.

Lines that are too short increase the number of eye movements, while long lines make it hard for the eye to stay on the correct line. The suitable length lies anywhere between 3 1/2 inches to 5 1/2 inches, depending on whether you are using double columns or a single column of text.

If your space is limited, use two columns rather than one that is more than 5 inches wide.

No right justification

Justified margins are even, with text aligned along the margin. Justified left margins are common practice and preferable. Headings and titles should be left-justified.

Ragged margins are uneven. Right-side margins should be ragged. This page has left justification with ragged right margins.

Ragged right margins make text easier to read because the eye can use the variation in line endings to help keep track as it moves down the page. Ragged right margins keep the spacing constant between words and between letters.

Columns

In printed text, two 3 1/2-inch wide columns are easier to read than text spread six inches across the page. A narrower single column (less than 5 1/2 inches but more than 3 1/2 inches) is easiest to read, but space constraints may require two columns.

Organization by Design

Find a unifying theme such as color or rhythm. Establish a visual pattern for different levels of headings or categories of information.

Use design elements to set off instructions from examples or history from updates. Break text up with subheadings, white space, and minor graphic accents.

Set a list apart with indenting or graphic accents like bullets, asterisks, or arrows. Only use numbers if you want to rank the items or prioritize them.

Put headings and subheadings at the left margin. Align graphics along a margin.

Use numbering systems

One obvious design tool is to use a scheme that uses characters and indentation to divide the material. Commonly used schemes combine alphabetic characters and numbers. Remember that a numerical scheme implies setting of priorities or hierarchical classification.

Avoid any organizing system that requires too many hierarchical levels. It is better to re-conceptualize or rewrite than to create an elaborate pyramid scheme.

Use other notations or signals if you do not mean to prioritize items in a list or table. Some schemes combine the following types of characters, available on any word-processor:

bullet •   star *

dash –   arrow >

Use headings to show architectural framework

Make your main headings stand out from the text by

- using bold type,
- using italics,
- using a different style for each level of heading,
- ranking the divisions in categories of equal importance.

Use hanging indents to provide more white space as a framework for information being presented and to show categories and hierarchies. This is a two-step hanging indent (giving it three levels):

Service of documents

Service by fax

Documents may be served by fax between the hours of 9:00 a.m. and 4:30 p.m. only.

Follow design guidelines for page layouts

The ingredients of good graphic design are:

structure – topical divisions,

type – size, face and style,

white space – margins and open spaces,

special treatment – for emphasis.

Special treatment includes the many simple design tools available on the word processor:

underline	italics
varied typefaces	capitalization
white space	quotation marks
boldface	indents
bullets	daggers

Image

Consider the image you want to relay to the reader. Design to project that image—whether it is casual, formal, youthful, or somber.

Type

Type styles have personalities. Some type styles look contemporary or friendly. Others are conservative or formal. You may choose a different typeface for your correspondence than the one you choose for your newsletter.

Typeface refers to the style of lettering. Roman typefaces have *serifs*—the finishing flourish, brush stroke, or tail.

The Gothic or Modern style eliminates the tails *(sans serif)* and has a stark appearance reminiscent of letters carved in stone.

You can choose between *serif* and *sans serif* typeface design. *Serif* type has a finishing flourish on many letters, which leads the eye to the next letter.

For Baby Boomers, *serif* is easier to read and is best used for text in most situations. *Sans-serif* types can be used for headings or other items to contrast with the text. You can reverse the pattern for younger readers. Use specially developed typefaces for internet text, or any text to be read on screen.

Use tables and visual aids

Visual aids can complement or even replace word descriptions.

Sometimes visual aids are a better way of presenting information. They can be used to show trends, directions, and interrelationships, or make comparisons.

Tables and graphs are effective for presenting data having numerical relationships and statistical data. Formulas explain mathematical relationships and processes easily.

Diagrams and maps are better than words to describe locations, routes, and geographical regions. Diagrams can also express concepts.

Photographs, drawings, and illustrations not only show what you mean to say, but shorten the number of words you need to say it. There are many graphic choices: bar charts, line graphs, pie charts, diagrams, line drawings, logos, maps, and clip art.

Legal Writing Design

Design faces the constraints of prescribed forms and traditional formats. Yet you can take full advantage of the options that are available to you to achieve an attractive visual presentation. Often the constraints, when examined more closely, are illusory.

For one example, the court rules may state that the forms may be varied to suit circumstances. So the format of the document may be changed to suit the content.

If the design of your document makes reading difficult, only committed readers will make the effort (the rest will telephone you for a summary explanation). Generally readers are motivated to read materials that appear easy-to-read, interesting, brief, and important. Your challenge is to give your document that appearance.

Good layout also reveals good organization of material. Design can assist the document organization by physically showing the connections or distinctions between ideas or parts.

Obstacles

Some of the obstacles to easy reading are:

- titles and headings that are centered,
- arbitrary internal spacing to force the text to fill a fixed depth or width (like justified right margins),
- inconsistent internal organization patterns,
- excessive use of indentation or spacing to place paragraph breaks where they are not needed,
- too much variety in the size, style, and weight of typefaces used for heading levels.

For other perspectives

There are two current resources that address design in the sense that it arises in correspondence and general communication in a professional setting:

- The Non-Designers Design Book, by Robin Williams
- Painting with Print: Incorporating concepts of typographic and layout design into the text of legal writing documents, by Ruth Anne Robbins, JALWD Fall 2004

Part Four: Resources
Writing Resources and Aids

Checklists and guidelines

It is helpful to have a checklist for any project. Choose a writing or an editing checklist that works for you or design your own and place it in a prominent or accessible location at your desk.

Grammar-checkers

Grammar checkers are incorporated in most writing software programs. They can review your writing for vocabulary, grammar, and style issues. *StyleWriter* does this and is also a plain-English editor.

Reference sources

You can keep the basic reference books at your desk to answer questions about spelling, grammar, and style. Or you can use resources on the Internet. You need to locate and bookmark a:

- dictionary
- dictionary of synonyms and antonyms
- legal dictionary
- style guide
- usage guide
- thesaurus
- guide to legal citations

Write your own

If your firm does not have a style guide or an approved firm style, volunteer to draft it. If one exists but its recommendations are out of style, volunteer to update it. Many firms now have precedent committees that review and update precedent documents. These committees are suitable forums for working out firm style. Find out if your firm has a precedent committee in your practice area.

Bibliography

Michelle M. Asprey, *Plain Language for Lawyers*, The Federation Press, Sydney, Aus., 1996

Robert W. Benson, "The End of Legalese: The Game is Over," The New York University Review of Law and Social Change, Vol. 13, 1984-1985, pp. 519-573

Mastering Legal Writing & Editing: How to Write Better & Faster, Clearlines, Chicago, Ill.

Bryan A. Garner, *The Elements of Legal Style*, Oxford University Press, New York, 1991

Ronald L. Goldfarb and James C. Raymond, *Clear Understandings: A Guide to Legal Writing*, Random House, 1982

Tom Goldstein and Jethro K. Lieberman, *The Lawyer's Guide to Writing Well*, McGraw-Hill Publishing Co., New York, 1989

Karen N. Gordon, *The Transitive Vampire: A Handbook of Grammar for the Innocent, the Eager and the Doomed*, Time Books, New York, 1984

Carl Felsenfeld and Alan Siegel, *Writing Contracts in Plain English*, West Publishing Co., St. Paul, Minn., 1981

Rudolf Flesch, *How to Write Plain English: A Book for Lawyers and Consumers*, Harper and Row, New York, 1979

Richard D. Lee, *Legal Opinions: Style, Structure, and Organization*, Law Society of Upper Canada CLE Materials

David Mellinkoff, *The Language of the Law*, Little, Brown and Company, Boston, 1963

David Mellinkoff, *Legal Writing: Sense and Nonsense*, West Publishing Co., St. Paul, Minn.., 1982

Timothy Perrin, *Better Writing for Lawyers*, The Law Society of Upper Canada, Toronto, Canada, 1990

Mary Bernard Ray and Jill J. Ramsfield, *Legal Writing: Getting it Right and Getting it Written*, West Publishing Co., St. Paul, Minn. 1987

Constance Rooke, *A Grammar Booklet for Lawyers or How Not to Dangle Your Participles in Public (and Other Good Advice)*, The Law Society of Upper Canada, Toronto, Canada, 1991

Henry Weihofen, *Legal Writing Style*, West Publishing Co., St. Paul, Minn., 1961

Joseph Williams, *Ten Lessons in Clarity and Grace*, Scott, Foresman and Co., Glenview, Ill., 1985

Richard C. Wydick, *Plain English for Lawyers*, Carolina Academic Press, Durham, N.C., 3rd ed. 1992

Blawgs (Legal Blogs)

Many law professors write regularly on legal writing. Here are some links:

- Suzanne Rowe and colleagues at the U of Oregon write for *The Oregon Bar Bulletin*. Go to http://www.osbar.org/publications/barpubs.html, click "Archives," and look for the monthly column "The Legal Writer."

- Gail Stephenson of Southern University Law Center has written a column titled "Gail's Grammar" in the Baton Rouge Bar Association's magazine since 1995. Go to http://www.brba.org/articles.cfm and click "View all" beside "Gail's Grammar" to access them all.

- Joe Kimble of Cooley Law School writes the "Plain Language" column in the *Michigan Bar Journal* since 1984. Go to http://www.michbar.org/generalinfo/plainenglish/columns.cfm.

- Wayne Schiess's legal-writing blog, http://www.utexas.edu/law/faculty/wschiess/legalwriting/

- Raymond Ward, the (new) legal writer, A collection of resources for lawyers and other writers. http://raymondpward.typepad.com/newlegalwriter/

- Mister Thorne, Set in Style, A skilled and experienced editor offers advice to those who could use one. http://misterthorne.org/set_in_style/

Glossary

analogy - a comparison of similarities between things otherwise not alike.

brainstorming - a technique aimed at getting as many creative solutions to a problem as possible: expressing any idea that comes to mind without analyzing it.

branching - a technique that consists of taking the kernel of an idea and drawing a diagram of a tree from it, with each related idea becoming a branch; the branches are later numbered by order of priority and used as your outline.

clause - a group of words containing a subject and a predicate and functioning as a member of a complex or compound sentence, a distinct article in a formal document.

cliché - a trite or overused expression or idea.

clustering - free-association of ideas that develop from your topic phrase using diagramming and free writing.

dialect - a regional variety of language distinguished by pronunciation, grammar or vocabulary; a variety of speech differing from the standard literary language or speech pattern of the culture in which it exists.

figure of speech - an expression, such as a metaphor or hyperbole, in which a nonliteral and intensive sense of a word or words is used to create a forceful, dramatic or illuminating image.

freewriting - like brainstorming but done individually and on paper; to freewrite start writing about your topic and don't lift your pen for a set period of time even if you run out of thoughts.

grammar - the study of language as a systematically composed body of words that exhibit discernible regularity of structure and arrangement into sentences; sometimes, the study of the classes of words, their inflections, and their functions and relations in the sentence

idiom - a speech form or expression of a given language that is peculiar to itself grammatically or that cannot be understood from the individual meanings of the elements; also, a specialized vocabulary used by a group of people.

jargon - a specialized or technical language of a trade, profession or group lexicon - the alphabetical arrangement of the words and their definitions in a language; a dictionary.

metaphor - a figure of speech in which a word or phrase literally relating to one kind of object or idea is used in place of another to suggest a likeness or analogy between them.

mnemonic - assisting or intended to assist memory; also of or relating to memory.

negative space - the white space on a page. Negative space is an important design element along with positive space, the text and artwork.

nominalization - word (a verb or other) or word group functioning as a noun.

nonstandard - a level of language usage that is usually avoided by educated speakers and writers.

parallelism - the quality or state of being parallel; resemblance, correspondence, recurrent syntactical similarities introduced for rhetorical effect.

recursive - a procedure that can repeat itself indefinitely or until a specified condition is met

rhetoric - the art of speaking or writing effectively, the study of the principles and rules of composition formulated by critics of ancient times; skill in the effective use of speech.

scenario - an account or synopsis of a projected course of action or events.

simile - a figure of speech comparing two unlike things and often introduced by the words like or as.

standard - conforming to established educated usage in speech or writing, as in Standard English.

syntax - a connected or orderly system, harmonious arrangements of parts or elements, the way in which words are put together to form phrases, clauses, or sentences, the part of grammar dealing with this.

term of art - a word or expression that has a precise meaning in some uses or is peculiar to a science, art, profession or subject.

usage - the actual or expressed way in which a language or its elements are used, interrelated, or pronounced.

Some definitions are adapted from *Webster's Ninth New Collegiate Dictionary*, (Merriam-Webster, 1983) or *The American Heritage Dictionary* (Houghton Mifflin Company, 1985).

About the Author

Cheryl Stephens, BA, LLB is a communication and training consultant and coach in Vancouver. She specializes in plain language and access issues in business, government, and law. She travels over all of North America providing training to individuals and groups on professional development and client relations for professional practices.

Cheryl is the author of two other Plain Language Wizardry books. Learn more about *Plain Language In Organizations: An Action Plan* and *Website Usability: A Plain Language Toolbox* at http://stores.lulu.com/email1058.

For more information about Cheryl, visit her web page, **CherylStephens.com**. And to learn more about plain language, browse to **PlainLanguage.com**.

0 1341 1389158 1